WOW!
ANCIENT HISTORY

**LONDON, NEW YORK,
MELBOURNE, MUNICH, AND DELHI**

For Tall Tree Ltd:
Editors Rob Colson, Jon Richards, and Jennifer Sanderson
Designers Malcolm Parchment and Ed Simkins

For Dorling Kindersley:
Senior editor Victoria Heyworth-Dunne
Senior designer Phillip Letsu

Managing editor Linda Esposito
Managing art editor Jim Green

Creative retouching Steve Willis
Picture research Louise Thomas

Category publisher Laura Buller

DK picture researcher Emma Shepherd
Production editor Andy Hilliard
Senior production controller Angela Graef

Jacket design Hazel Martin
Jacket editor Matilda Gollon
Design development manager Sophia M Tampakopoulos Turner
Development team Yumiko Tahata

First published in Great Britain in 2011 by
Dorling Kindersley Limited,
80 Strand, London, WC2R 0RL
Penguin Group (UK)

10 9 8 7 6 5 4 3 2 1
001–179075–July/11

A CIP catalogue record for this book
is available from the British Library

ISBN: 978-1-40536-511-6

Printed and bound by Leo, China

Discover more at
www.dk.com

WOW!
ANCIENT
HISTORY

1

2

3

4

Contents

ISHTAR GATE
This image of a lion once adorned the Processional Way in Babylon. Built in 575 BCE, the road linked the main entrance of the city, the Ishtar Gate, with the ziggurat temple of the chief Babylonian god, Marduk.

The Middle East

FERTILE CRESCENT

A group of people that farms the land to create surpluses of food, lives in cities, has a society with a hierarchy, and is ruled by some form of government is said to be a "civilization". Civilizations emerged gradually at different times around the world. The first civilizations developed in the Middle East, where farming first began around 10,000 years ago, in a place called Mesopotamia.

Mesopotamia

▶ HUNTER-GATHERERS

Farming first started as a result of climate change at the end of the last ice age. Before that, people were hunter-gatherers, moving from place to place in search of food. However, the new weather conditions changed the previous distribution of plants, which people had been familiar with. It is believed that people began planting wild seeds and tubers as a way of guaranteeing their food supply.

Bow, arrows, and a gathering bag used by prehistoric hunter-gatherers

▼ CULTIVATION OF PLANTS

Early farming involved the simple gathering and planting of wild seeds. The first crops to be cultivated on a significant scale were emmer wheat, einkorn wheat, barley, lentils, peas, bitter vetch, chick peas, and flax. Together, these are known as the eight founder crops. Selective breeding of these plants allowed early farmers to produce bigger crops with a greater yield. Some of this food could be stored for later use.

Modern wheat

Selective breeding has created plump seeds

Einkorn wheat

Wild wheat has small seeds that hold less flour

▲ THE FERTILE CRESCENT

The Fertile Crescent, where the first farmers appeared around 10,000 years ago, is an area of land that stretches in an arc through parts of modern Israel, Lebanon, Syria, Turkey, and Iraq. There were two main factors that made this stretch of the Middle East ripe for agriculture: firstly, it had a climate with warm temperatures and reliable rainfall; secondly, it had a wide range of plants and animals that were suitable for domestication.

▲ DOMESTICATION OF ANIMALS

Once people discovered that cultivation provided them with a secure supply of crops, they tried to find equally secure supplies of meat. This led to the domestication of animals in around 8000 BCE, beginning with sheep and followed soon after by goats, pigs, and cattle. The "Standard of Ur" (shown here) dates from 2600–2400 BCE and has images of cattle, sheep, and goats being prepared for a major feast.

▼ MESOPOTAMIA

Farming allowed people to settle down in permanent communities in places where there was regular rainfall. The development of irrigation – the process of digging channels to bring water from rivers to fields such as these modern channels on the Euphrates – meant that people could move to dryer areas. In around 6000 BCE, people migrated onto the flood plains of the Tigris and Euphrates rivers. This area would become known as Mesopotamia, meaning the "land between two rivers".

▼ FIRST TOWNS

The development of settled farming communities led to the emergence of the first towns, such as Ur (shown below). These were located in a part of Mesopotamia known as Sumer and appeared during the Ubaid Period (5900–4300 BCE). They consisted of simple houses made of sun-dried mud bricks. There was usually a temple at the centre of the town. The town's leaders were also its religious elite, controlling food supply and worship.

▼ SOCIAL DIVISIONS

As farming techniques became more advanced, so hierarchies began to develop. Irrigation was complicated, labour-intensive work that needed to be organized. Successful farming also created surplus food that could be stored as insurance against a poor harvest. These food stores were the first forms of wealth in human societies. The people who organized the labour and controlled the food stores became the first chiefs.

▼ CRAFTS

In hunter-gatherer times, people could not create more goods than they could carry. Farming and the creation of surpluses allowed people to settle and to collect possessions and practise different activities, such as arts and crafts. One of the earliest crafts was pottery making. Pots, such as these from the Ubaid Period, were invented as a way of storing food. Over time they became more sophisticated.

Highly decorated pots were symbols of high social status

9

FIRST CITIES

During the Uruk Period from 4300–3100 BCE, the towns of Sumer in southern Mesopotamia grew into the world's first cities. This made Sumer the world's first urban civilization. Each city was a separate state with its own government, but all the Sumerian people shared a culture, speaking the same language and worshipping the same gods. The largest and most powerful of these early city-states was Uruk, which may have had as many as 50,000 inhabitants at its peak.

▼ THE ROLE OF RELIGION

Religion was very important in Sumerian society. At the heart of each city was a temple where ceremonies were performed to please the gods and ensure a good harvest. As food was seen as the property of the gods, it was stored at the temple and distributed to the people by the religious leaders, or *ensis*.

▶ KINGS

In the third millennium BCE, Sumer's religious leaders were gradually replaced by kings (*lugals*). The first kings were probably military leaders who remained in charge in peacetime. The king had three roles – he was the head of government, the religious leader, and the city's chief warrior.

This gold helmet belonged to Meskalamdug who ruled the city of Ur in around 2500 BCE

Statue of an *ensi*, one of the priest-governors who ruled early Sumerian cities

Cuneiform was written by making marks in a wet clay tablet using a reed stylus

▶ WRITING

The Sumerians developed the world's first writing system in around 3400 BCE. To begin with, it was made up of a simple set of symbols but, by 2900 BCE, a complex writing system, called cuneiform, had been developed, consisting of hundreds of different symbols.

◀ LAW CODES

To keep control of their subjects in the cities, the Sumerians created the first law codes. These codes told the people what practices where forbidden and what the punishments were for law-breakers. Perhaps more importantly, they also showed the gods how fair and just the kings who issued the codes were, thus maintaining the gods' favour.

Terracotta cone inscribed with details of laws made in 2360 BCE

▼ ART AND BRONZE

As Sumer's urban society became more complex, so did its art. Clay was Sumer's most abundant material and was used for the majority of early artworks. Later on, as trade expanded, stone, wood, metal, precious stones, and bronze became available. The Sumerians were the first people to master bronze, using it to make weapons and tools.

The Sumerians created numerous bronze artworks, such as this statue of a religious figure

▼ WARFARE

Weapons made of bronze were much harder, sharper, and longer-lasting than any that had been made before. They proved particularly useful in the third millennium BCE, as Sumer's cities grew and came into conflict over resources. Large city-states, such as Kish, Uruk, and Ur, vied for supremacy, conquering and taking over rivals. This led to the establishment of the first empires.

This box, dating from around 2600–2400 BCE, shows a Sumerian army from the city of Ur

◀ SEALS

The Sumerians used stone cylinder seals to mark ownership of their goods. Usually worn around the neck, the seal was engraved with a pattern that could be identified with its owner. The seal would be rolled over a piece of wet clay, forming a unique impression, almost like a signature.

KINGS AND EMPIRES

In the 24th century BCE, Sumer was conquered by a new regional power from northern Mesopotamia, Akkad. The Akkadian king Sargon (2334–2279 BCE) took over a vast stretch of territory from the Mediterranean Sea to the Persian Gulf, creating the world's first empire. It crumbled a couple of centuries later and was replaced by a new empire centred on the Sumerian city of Ur. In time, this too was conquered by the Elamite people.

▼ ROYAL BIRTH?

Sargon may have been the master of the Middle East, but his origins were far more humble – he was the son of a date farmer. After he came to power, a legend was created, perhaps to help with his claim to the throne. This legend stated that he was, in fact, the illegitimate son of a royal priestess. She had tried to get rid of him by placing him in a basket on the Euphrates (much like Moses in the Bible). He was then discovered by a royal gardener, who brought him up as his own child.

▲ THE FIRST DYNASTY

Ruling from his capital at Agade, the site of which has never been found, Sargon established Mesopotamia's first successful dynasty. His sons consolidated his achievements, while his grandson, Naram-Sin, built the Akkadian empire up to the height of its power. Naram-Sin was the first Middle Eastern ruler to refer to himself as a god – this stone tablet shows Naram-Sin as a god-king standing above his soldiers. However, following his death in 2029 BCE, his empire went into decline as the Mesopotamian cities revolted.

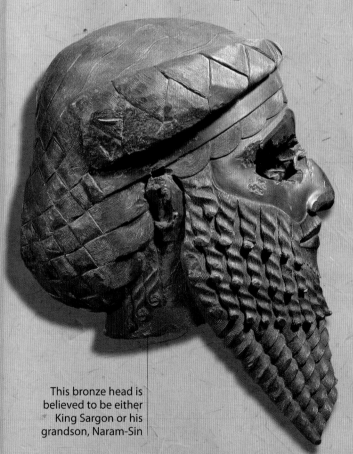

This bronze head is believed to be either King Sargon or his grandson, Naram-Sin

This stone plaque depicts Ishtar, the Babylonian version of the Akkadian goddess Inanna

▶ THE FIRST AUTHOR

Sargon appointed his daughter, Enheduanna, as the high priestess at the temple of Nanna, the Moon god, in the city of Ur. Over time, Enheduanna came to revere Nanna's daughter, Inanna, the goddess of love, fertility, and warfare, above all other deities. She travelled widely, promoting the worship of the goddess by writing hymns in her honour. Versions of these hymns still survive, making Enheduanna the first author in history whose name we know.

Imprint from a
cylinder seal shows
Ur-Nammu (seated)
and his high priest

▲ RISE OF UR

The Akkadian empire crumbled almost as quickly as it had been built. Naram-Sin's son, Shar-Kali-Sharri, spent much of his 25-year reign fending off attacks by foreign tribes. After his death, the region's city-states jostled for power. In 2112 BCE, Ur-Nammu, the king of the Sumerian city of Ur, took control of Sumeria and Akkad. He built a new empire covering much of Mesopotamia and the neighbouring civilization of Elam.

▶ ZIGGURATS

Ur-Nammu's reign saw the creation of the first ziggurats – giant step pyramids that towered above the landscape. Unlike the pyramids of Egypt, which were built around the same time, these were not tombs but places of worship, designed to reach up to the heavens. Made of mud bricks, each ziggurat was topped with a temple where it was believed the gods slept at night. The practice of ziggurat building was continued by the Assyrians and the Babylonians, who were responsible for the Etemananki Ziggurat in Babylon.

Access to the top
temple was by
stairways and ramps

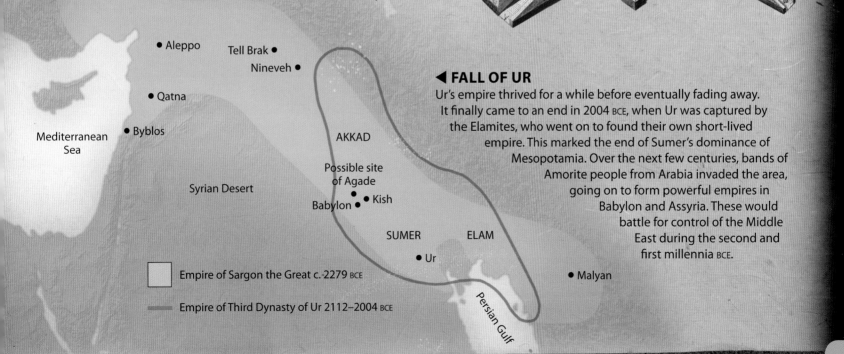

◀ FALL OF UR

Ur's empire thrived for a while before eventually fading away. It finally came to an end in 2004 BCE, when Ur was captured by the Elamites, who went on to found their own short-lived empire. This marked the end of Sumer's dominance of Mesopotamia. Over the next few centuries, bands of Amorite people from Arabia invaded the area, going on to form powerful empires in Babylon and Assyria. These would battle for control of the Middle East during the second and first millennia BCE.

Aleppo
Tell Brak
Nineveh
Qatna
Byblos
Mediterranean Sea
Syrian Desert
AKKAD
Possible site of Agade
Babylon • Kish
SUMER
ELAM
Ur
Malyan

Persian Gulf

☐ Empire of Sargon the Great c. 2279 BCE

— Empire of Third Dynasty of Ur 2112–2004 BCE

ASSYRIA VS BABYLON

In the first millennium BCE, two great powers, Assyria and Babylon, fought for control of the Middle East. The Assyrians conquered Babylon, Egypt, and Elam. However, when the great Assyrian king, Arshurbanipal, died in 627 BCE, Babylon fought back. It took control of Assyria and built up its own empire under King Nebuchadnezzar II (605–562 BCE). However, following his reign, Babylon was invaded by Persia and its power melted away.

▼ ASSYRIAN ARMY
The Assyrians were famously fearsome warriors. Their soldiers were among the first to use iron weapons. This gave them a huge advantage over their rivals, whose weapons were made of softer bronze. The Assyrians fought with swords and spears, and used battering rams to break down city walls. Their main weapon was the bow. Large companies of 100 bowmen would use these to shoot iron-tipped arrows at their enemies.

PROPAGANDA ▶
The Assyrians liked to boast about their victories. Their palaces were covered with battle scenes showing their military might. They did this both to celebrate their successes and as propaganda, showing the dangers of challenging Assyrian power. This wall relief shows the Assyrian king Arshurbanipal enjoying a victory banquet.

▲ CHARIOTS
During the early years of their empire, the Assyrians rode into battle on chariots, like the one depicted here. But these were difficult to use on uneven ground, and so over time they were replaced by soldiers on horseback. Each horse had two riders – one to hold the reins and one to fight the enemy using a spear or a bow and arrow.

NINEVEH ▶
This mythical creature, which was part bull, part bird, and part man, was known as the Lamassu. It adorned the walls of the palace at Nineveh, the Assyrian capital. Nineveh was founded in the second millennium BCE as a ceremonial centre for Ishtar, the goddess of love and war. Its population grew to more than 100,000, making it one of the world's largest cities at the time.

◀ GREAT LIBRARY
Arshurbanipal had a reputation as a cruel, ruthless leader, but he was also a great patron of learning. He built up a vast library in Nineveh of more than 20,000 cuneiform tablets. It contained religious texts, official contracts, ancient legends, royal decrees, and administrative letters. After Nineveh was sacked, the library was buried and rediscovered only in the 19th century.

EPIC OF GILGAMESH ▲
Among the tablets found in Arshurbanipal's library were ones relating the *Epic of Gilgamesh*, one of the earliest works of literature. It tells the story of Gilgamesh, king of Uruk, including his battle with the "Bull of Heaven", shown here, and his fruitless search for immortality. The epic also contains a "flood myth", which is very similar to the story of Noah's Ark in the Bible.

BABYLON ▶
The Babylonian empire was centred on Babylon, which Nebuchadnezzar II turned into the region's finest city. Entry into Babylon was through eight gates, such as the Ishtar Gate, which was decorated with images of animals, including aurochs (shown here). Soon after Nebuchadnezzar's death, Babylon was conquered by Persia and the empire crumbled.

◀ HANGING GARDENS
Nebuchadnezzar II's most famous creation was the Hanging Gardens of Babylon. Supposedly built to ease his wife's homesickness, the gardens were designed to imitate the mountains of her homeland in Persia. They were considered so spectacular that they were named one of the Seven Wonders of the World.

HAMMURABI'S LAW CODE ▶
An early Babylonian king, called Hammurabi (1792–1750 BCE), created a code made up of 282 laws to show what a just ruler he was. These laws dealt with all aspects of society and spelt out penalties for anyone who broke the law. This picture shows Hammurabi receiving the code from the Babylonian Sun god, Shamash.

MIDDLE EASTERN FIRSTS

The Mesopotamians were the great pioneers of the ancient world. They were the first people to develop farming, the first to live in cities, and the first to use vehicles with wheels. They were also the first people to devise a system of mathematics and to make detailed observations of the night sky. We know a great deal about the Mesopotamians because, perhaps most importantly, they were the first to record their achievements using a written language.

The Sumerians used wheeled chariots to transport soldiers

▶ FIRST SAIL BOATS

Although the Sumerians did not invent boats, it is believed they were the first people to think of moving them using sails. These sails would have been made of cloth or animal skins. Boats allowed the Sumerians to travel much more widely and quickly than ever before. They also allowed later peoples, such as the Phoenicians, to create vast trading networks.

This 6,000-year-old model boat from Sumer is the earliest evidence for the use of sails

▶ FIRST WHEELS

No one knows exactly when the wheel was invented, but it was in use in Sumer by around 3500 BCE. The Sumerians used the wheel in two ways: vertically, on carts, chariots, and other vehicles, and horizontally to make pots. The Sumerians' invention of the potter's wheel allowed them to make pots in greater volume, and of a much higher quality than ever before.

▶ FIRST NUMBERS

The development of numbers grew out of a need to keep accurate records. The early Sumerians used tokens marked with pictures to record the contents of storage vessels – for example, a picture of two ovals might mean two bottles of oil. From this, the concept of abstract numbers gradually emerged. By around 2000 BCE, a fully developed system of mathematics had been created.

Cuneiform numbers

▼ FIRST ARMIES

The rise of the Sumerian civilization in the fourth millennium BCE saw the creation of the world's first organized armies, as the expanding cities came into conflict with one another over resources. On the battlefield, the Sumerian armies lined up behind a wall of shields and fought with spears, daggers, and axes.

▶ FIRST WRITING

In the fourth millennium BCE, the Sumerians developed cuneiform – the world's first writing system. It proved highly successful and was later adopted by the Assyrian and Babylonian civilizations. However, in around 600 BCE, cuneiform began to die out following the introduction of the Aramaic alphabet. It had completely fallen out of use by the first century BCE.

Sumerian soldiers wore helmets made of bronze or leather and fought with bronze-tipped spears

▶ FIRST TIME KEEPERS

The Sumerians created the first calendar by dividing the year into 12 parts based on the movements of the Moon. Their calendar was refined by the Babylonians. They made detailed studies of the night sky, which they divided into 12 sections named after constellations. This concept has passed down to today as the signs of the Zodiac.

By watching the waxing and waning of the Moon, the Mesopotamians kept track of the passage of the year

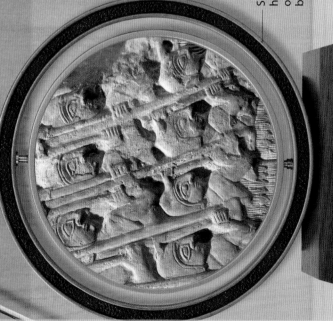

BIBLE LANDS

The Hebrew people emerged in the Middle East towards the end of the second millennium BCE. They were not the most powerful civilization of the age, but they would prove much more influential than any of their contemporaries. The beliefs they developed formed the basis of three major religions – Judaism, Christianity, and Islam – which are followed by billions of people around the world today.

❶ ORIGINS

According to the Bible, the Hebrews were nomadic, which means they moved around. Following a period of slavery in Egypt, they were guided by their leader Moses (left) to Canaan in the Middle East, where they settled. However, there is no archaeological evidence for this story. In fact, some historians believe the Hebrews were not migrants, but descendants of the native Canaanite people.

❷ ONE GOD

The Hebrews were monotheists, which means they worshipped just one god, rather than many gods as most of the region's other peoples did. The Hebrews' holy book, the Bible, forbade them from making images of their god. According to the Bible, when the Hebrews made a golden calf (below) to represent their deity, they were severely punished by their leader, Moses.

❸ INVENTORS OF THE ALPHABET

The part of the Middle East that corresponds to modern-day Israel and the Palestinian territories was first settled in the third millennium BCE by the Canaanites. The Canaanites often fought the region's other people, including the Philistines and the Hebrews. Like the Hebrews, they had a profound impact on future generations, developing a simple alphabet. This evolved into the system of letters we use today.

❹ HEBREW KINGS

At first, the Hebrews were divided into tribes ruled by leaders called "judges". However, threats from outside forces eventually led them to unite into a single kingdom, Israel, behind a single king. According to the Bible, the first king was Saul (ruled 1020–1006 BCE). He was succeeded by David, who conquered the Canaanite settlement of Jerusalem and made it his capital.

Statue of David and the head of Goliath

a	h	y	k	i	r	s	t
b							
g							
d	e		m	n			
w							
z							

18

5 SOLOMON

David was succeeded by his son, Solomon, who constructed the Hebrews' holiest site, the Temple in Jerusalem. This contained the Ark of the Covenant, a giant stone box (shown left) holding the stone tablets on which the set of laws called the Ten Commandments were written. After Solomon's death, the kingdom split into two parts – Judah and Israel.

6 DESTRUCTION OF ISRAEL

In the early centuries of the first millennium BCE, the Hebrews came under Egyptian and then Assyrian control. When Israel and Judah came into conflict with each other in the eighth century BCE, Judah asked Assyria for help. Assyria's response was brutal, destroying Israel in 722 BCE and moving its population to the east, as shown in this wall relief from an Assyrian palace.

7 CONQUEST OF JUDAH

In 586 BCE, the Babylonians marched into Judah, flattening the Temple in Jerusalem and moving the population to Babylon. The Bible portrays the Babylonian king, Nebuchadnezzar II, as an evil tyrant who was sent mad by God for his sins against the Hebrews, as in this picture by the 19th-century artist, William Blake. In truth, he was probably no more ruthless than any other ruler of the time.

8 EXPULSION

The Babylonians were eventually overthrown by the Persians, who allowed the Jews (as the Hebrews were now known) to return to their homeland. They built a new temple, but by the first century CE they had come under Roman control. Jewish revolts against Roman rule led to the destruction of the Second Temple and the expulsion of the Jews from the region. Today only the western wall of the temple (shown here) still stands.

THE PHOENICIANS

The Phoenicians emerged on the Middle East's west coast in the second millennium BCE. These skilled sailors may have been the first people to sail out of sight of land. They spent the next 1,000 years establishing trade routes right across the Mediterranean. They did not just transport goods, however, but also new ideas and technologies.

▼ TRADE

Phoenician power was based not on conquest, but trade. They built up a great commercial network, dealing in a vast range of goods, including silver and copper from Spain, grain and iron from Italy, and gold, ivory, and slaves from tropical Africa. Their desire for new markets saw them sail farther than any of the region's people had done before.

ALPHABET ▲

The Phoenicians were the descendants of the Canaanites, who developed the world's first alphabet. This was improved upon by the Phoenicians, and spread through their trading network. It was passed on to the Greeks, who in turn passed on a refined version (with vowels) to the Romans. It forms the basis of the alphabet we use today.

▶ SHIP BUILDERS

The Phoenicians were great ship builders. For much of their history, they built long ships known as galleys, powered by a line of rowers. However, in around the seventh century BCE, they invented a new vessel, the bireme. This used two lines of rowers, one above the other, and a sail. Together, these allowed the Phoenicians to travel even farther and faster.

▶ IN THE PURPLE

Of all the goods traded by the Phoenicians, the most valuable was a rich purple dye known as Tyrian purple (named after the city of Tyre). It was made by boiling up the bodies of a rare type of sea snail and was highly prized. At times it was said to have "cost its own weight in silver". Only high-status individuals could afford materials coloured with this dye.

This is a Phoenician carving of a sphinx, an Egyptian mythical creature

▲ GREAT MIXERS

The Phoenician trading network was one of the great cultural exchange systems. Along with olive oil, jewellery, and timber, the Phoenicians also passed on new technologies, religious beliefs, and artistic styles. The Phoenician language was particularly influential. Many places across the Mediterranean today have names derived from Phoenician, including Cadiz (Gadir), Malta (Malat), and Spain (I-Shapan).

▼ CITY-STATES

The Phoenicians founded a number of city-states. The most important were Tyre and Carthage, which were packed with warehouses filled with trade goods, such as these. These cities never united to form a single empire. Instead, they remained rivals and would only occasionally join together against a common enemy.

▲ SERVING OTHER MASTERS

The years from 1200–800 BCE marked the high point of Phoenician influence. After this time, however, they were dominated by other powers. First Assyria took control, then Babylon, and then Persia, before Phoenicia was finally conquered by Alexander the Great in 332 BCE. It was absorbed into the Greek-speaking Hellenistic world and many Phoenician cities, such as Sabatha in North Africa (shown here), were abandoned.

PERSIAN EMPIRE

When King Cyrus came to the Persian throne in 559 BCE, Persia was just a small state controlled by the neighbouring Median empire. Twenty years later it had become a great empire, having conquered both the Median and Babylonian empires. Cyrus had earned himself a new nickname "The Great". The Persian empire reached its peak under Darius I (521–486 BCE), when it was a cultural melting pot of Greek, Indian, Mesopotamian, and Egyptian influences. However, in the fourth century BCE it was conquered by another "great", Alexander.

▼ TAKING THE THRONE
Persian legends tell that when Cyrus was a child, his grandfather King Astyages tried to have him killed after a dream in which Cyrus overthrew him. However, the servant sent to kill Cyrus could not do it. When Aystages discovered the deception, he tricked the servant into eating his own son at a banquet. Cyrus grew up to seize the throne, just as the dream had predicted.

▲ ZOROASTRIANISM
During his reign, Cyrus the Great helped to popularize a new religion, known as Zoroastrianism. Founded in around 1000 BCE by Zoroaster, a Persian philosopher, it was one of the world's first monotheistic religions. Its followers worship just one god, Ahura Mazda. This relief sculpture from the Adapana Palace shows Ahura Mazda, the Zoroastrian deity. His counterpart is Angra Mainyu, the evil spirit.

▲ CYRUS THE GREAT
Though ferocious in battle, Cyrus the Great had a reputation for fairness and for respecting the customs and religions of the people he conquered. Unlike many other leaders, he did not banish conquered people after a victory. In fact, he even allowed the Jews to return to their homeland following their earlier deportation by the Babylonians. Cyrus's tomb (shown above) still stands in his capital city, Pasagardae.

The Cyrus Cylinder lists all the good deeds Cyrus supposedly performed

▶ PROPAGANDA
Like many other Middle Eastern rulers, Cyrus used propaganda to proclaim his greatness. One example of this is a clay cylinder created just after the conquest of Babylon. It is inscribed with cuneiform script and states what a great king Cyrus is, how bad the previous Babylonian king had been, and how pleased the gods are with Cyrus.

▼ PERSEPOLIS

The Persian empire's largest city was Persepolis. It was built for Darius I, who seized the throne in 521 BCE. At the city's centre was the vast Adapana Palace. Its walls were covered with pictures of lions and bulls, which were symbols of imperial might. This frieze from the 100 Columns Palace in Persepolis shows people taking part in the *Nowruz* (Persian New Year) celebrations.

▼ GREEK RESISTANCE

In the early fifth century BCE, Persia seemed ready to expand into Europe. However, in great battles at Marathon (490 BCE), Thermopylae (480 BCE), and Salamis (480 BCE), the Greeks halted their progress. According to legend, after the Battle of Marathon (shown below) a messenger ran 42 km (26 miles) to Athens to bring news of the Greek victory. Eventually, the Persians were expelled from the Greek peninsula altogether.

▲ CONQUEST BY ALEXANDER

For all their military power, the Persians succumbed quickly to Alexander the Great in the fourth century BCE. The Greek armies took Persepolis in 330 BCE and the city was looted and burned by Greek troops. Buried beneath the foundations of Persepolis, before it was sacked by the Greeks, this gold plate boasted of Darius's military might.

THE SPICE ROUTE

In the first millennium BCE, getting spices, such as black pepper and cinnamon, from their place of origin in Southeast Asia to the markets of the Middle East, Egypt, and Europe was a lengthy and difficult process. This made spices extremely expensive. However, the long-distance trade in spices helped to establish communication channels between Europe, India, Southeast Asia, and China. At the centre of this trade lay the Arabian peninsula.

❶ **EARLY DAYS**

No one knows exactly when the spice trade began, but it seems to have been surprisingly early. There are reports of cloves, which are native to the Moluccas (Spice Islands) in Indonesia, being used in Sumeria in 2500 BCE. In the second millennium BCE, the Egyptian pharaoh Ramses II (died 1213 BCE) was buried with black peppercorns from India inserted into his nostrils.

❷ **NABATAEANS**

In the first millennium BCE, the spice trade in the Middle East was controlled by the Nabataeans, a people from Northern Arabia. The Nabataeans established camel caravan routes that linked up the oasis settlements of the Arabian peninsula. As well as spices, the Nabataeans also dealt in animal skins, ivory, and gold from East Africa, as well as incense from India.

The Ebers Papyrus from 1550 BCE is an Egyptian medical text listing remedies including the Southeast Asian spices cassia and cinnamon

❸ **PETRA**

Founded in the sixth century BCE, the Nabataean capital was the city of Petra. Located in a steep mountain valley, it became the centre of their caravan trade. Here, the Nabataeans carved houses, temples, and tombs out of the valley's pink-coloured rock. Though deep in the dry desert, Petra thrived because the Nabataeans managed to create complicated systems for storing water from flash floods for use in times of drought.

❹ BEYOND THE SIQ

Petra occupied an easily defended site protected by high valley walls. Entrance was along a long gorge known as the Siq (shown here). It had sides up to 200 m (650 ft) high and was less than 3 m (10 ft) wide in parts. Free from outside interference, the city thrived until the second century CE when it was finally conquered by the Romans. The city was abandoned following an earthquake in 363 CE and was not rediscovered until the 19th century.

❺ PUNT

Southeast Asia was not the only source of exotic produce for the Mediterranean civilizations. It is known that ancient Egypt also imported gold, ivory, and animal skins from the African kingdom of Punt. Punt was considered such an important contact that, in the fifteenth century BCE, the Egyptian queen Hatshepsut sent a trading mission there. This picture shows one of the boats used in the expedition. The site of Punt has never been found.

❻ SEA TRADE

While the Nabataeans of North Arabia dominated the land routes, the maritime trade of spice in the first millennium BCE was controlled by people from southern Arabia. These traders were able to sail as far as India's west coast by taking advantage of their knowledge of "secret" trade winds that greatly reduced journey times. Much of the spice trade flowed through Kerala in southwest India, and on by land and sea east to China and west to Europe.

❼ A DANGEROUS BUSINESS

Spice traders were keen to protect their lucrative business. To stop people trying to take over their trade, and to remind their customers how difficult the spices were to obtain, the traders invented elaborate legends. This also helped to keep their prices high. One story from the fifth century BCE, reported by the Greek author Herodotus (shown here), told how the spice cassia grew in lakes protected by giant bat-like creatures.

❽ ALEXANDRIA AND ROME

After its foundation in the fourth century BCE, the city of Alexandria became one of the Mediterranean's greatest centres of commerce. It was also a major player in the spice trade, although this was still dominated by Arab traders. That changed when Rome took over Alexandria in 80 BCE and set about taking control of the spice routes. The discovery of the trade winds allowed Rome to trade directly with India, using Roman sailing vessels (shown here) and ended the Arab spice monopoly.

China

Petra
Alexandria • Arabian • India
Peninsula Kerala
Aden Moluccas

KARNAK
These giant columns form part of the ancient Egyptian temple complex of Karnak in the city of Thebes. Dedicated to the god Amun, most of the temple was constructed in the 14th century BCE.

26

Africa

ANCIENT EGYPT

Emerging around 7,000 years ago along the banks of the Nile in North Africa, Egypt grew into one of the greatest civilizations of the ancient world, lasting for an astounding 3,000 years. During this time, Egypt was ruled by a succession of royal families, called dynasties, led by the pharaoh. The history of Egypt is usually divided into three main periods, known as the Old, Middle, and New Kingdoms.

❶ EARLY EGYPT

The first small settlements on the banks of the Nile were founded around 5000 BCE. These grew steadily, and by 3500 BCE, a number of kingdoms had emerged. Competition and warfare between the kingdoms saw them join together until there were just two left: Upper Egypt in the south and Lower Egypt in the north. In 3100 BCE, Pharaoh Narmer conquered Lower Egypt to create a single kingdom.

❷ EARLY DYNASTIC PERIOD

Between 3100–2650 BCE, many of the major hallmarks of Egyptian culture emerged, including their writing system (hieroglyphics), their religion, and their main art styles. The role of the pharaoh became increasingly important, and his distinctive mode of dress was developed, involving a striped headdress, a fake beard, and a kilt. Egypt's cities began to grow much larger at this time.

An ivory board used to play the game senet, in which players had to negotiate their way through the *duat*, or underworld

Red Sea

Pi-Ramses
Nile Delta
Memphis
Giza
LOWER EGYPT
Eastern Desert
Thebes
Nubian Desert
UPPER EGYPT

❶

Ceremonial plate showing pharaoh Narmer conquering Lower Egypt

❷

Pharaoh Mentuhotep II of the 11th Dynasty

❸

❹

Senusret III was one of the most powerful of the Middle Kingdom pharaohs

❺

❸ OLD KINGDOM

Egypt's first period of greatness began in 2649 BCE. High agricultural production created great wealth for the pharaohs, allowing them to fund lavish building projects, such as the huge stone pyramids. The pharaoh was regarded as a semi-divine being and an incarnation of the falcon god, Horus (shown here). Pharaohs ruled from the capital at Memphis.

❹ FIRST INTERMEDIATE PERIOD

The Old Kingdom ended in 2134 BCE after a series of poor harvests. The inability of the pharaohs to prevent the catastrophe weakened their authority. Local leaders tried to usurp the throne, proclaiming themselves pharaohs and engaging in civil war. Eventually, the 11th Dynasty of Upper Egypt emerged victorious and the capital was moved to Thebes.

❺ MIDDLE KINGDOM

Stability returned from 2040–1640 BCE, but the pharaohs had lost a good deal of prestige through their failure to prevent the famines. No pyramids on the scale seen in the Old Kingdom were built. Egypt conquered the southern kingdom of Nubia, where there were valuable gold reserves, as well as supplies of ebony, ivory, and animal skins. The capital was moved back to Memphis.

❻ SECOND INTERMEDIATE PERIOD

After several centuries of calm, the Hyksos people from the Middle East conquered Lower Egypt in 1640 BCE, prompting the Nubians in the south (shown here) to revolt. The Hyksos invasion had its benefits, however, as they brought with them new technologies from the more advanced Middle East, including wheeled vehicles, bronze weapons, and domesticated animals.

❼ NEW KINGDOM

In 1532 BCE, the Hyksos were forced out of Egypt, marking the start of the New Kingdom, when Egypt would reach the height of its power. Egyptian territory was expanded north into the Middle East and south into Nubia, and great temple complexes honouring the pharaohs were erected, such as the one at Karnak (shown here).

❽ HATSHEPSUT

Pharaohs were usually male, but occasionally women took charge. Hatshepsut became pharaoh in 1508 BCE when her husband, Thutmose II, died. She was very successful, reigning for 21 years and sending a famous trade mission to Punt. However, after her death, her successor, Thutmose III, tried to have all mention of her erased and had all her monuments torn down.

Though female, Hatshepsut still wore the traditional male clothing of the pharaoh, including the false beard

❾ AKHENATEN

The pharaoh Amenhotep IV (1351–1334 BCE) tried to replace Egypt's religion with a new cult centred on just one deity, the Sun god Aten. He even renamed himself Akhenaten in honour of the new god. Despite the support of his wife, Nefertiti (shown here), all of Akhenaten's changes were reversed upon his death.

❿ RAMSES II

One of the last great pharaohs, Ramses II (1279–1213 BCE) ruled for 66 years. He reclaimed much of the territory lost following Akhenaten's reign. He erected giant monuments to his own achievements, such as the temple at Abu Simbel shown here. He also established a new capital – Pi-Ramses.

⓫ LATE PERIOD

The high point of Ramses II's reign was followed by a steady decline. By 1000 BCE, all the territory won by the pharaohs of the New Kingdom had been lost. In 332 BCE, Egypt succumbed to the armies of Alexander the Great. When Cleopatra, shown here, died in 30 BCE, Egypt became a Roman province.

GIFT OF THE NILE

The world's longest river, stretching for some 6,400 km (4,000 miles) from the African tropics to the Mediterranean Sea, the Nile was the great ribbon of life flowing through the heart of ancient Egypt. With much of the country covered in inhospitable desert, civilization grew up alongside the river's banks. Every aspect of Egyptian daily life depended on the river. The Egyptians relied on it for water supplies, for transport, and to fertilize the soil. Every summer, the river flooded, depositing a thick layer of nutrient-rich silt on the land either side where farmers planted their crops. When the land was submerged, no farming was done. Instead, people worked on building projects for the pharaoh, erecting great temples and monuments.

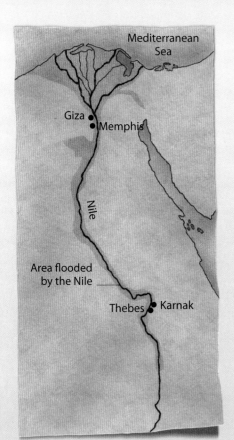

◄ ANNUAL FLOOD
In August and September, high rainfall near the Nile's source caused the waters to rise rapidly. Eventually, the river burst its banks, flooding the surrounding area. This was the most important time of year for the Egyptians. A strong flood meant a good harvest; a weak one might mean a poor harvest and possibly even a famine.

▼ BOATS
Boats were used for a variety of purposes, including trade, warfare, and construction, carrying goods, troops, and stone up and down the river. They were also used for fishing and to carry the deceased to their tombs. Pharaohs would ride on large ceremonial boats on important occasions. Model boats were often buried in the tombs of important people for use in the afterlife.

▼ JEWELLERY
People wore jewellery to honour the gods. Amulets in the shape of scarab beetles, like the one below, were common. Scarab beetles were seen as a sign of rebirth and were associated with the god Khepri, who pushed the Sun across the sky, just like a dung beetle pushing its ball of dung.

▼ FARMING
The farming year in ancient Egypt began following the annual flood when the newly fertile soil was ploughed and planted. At harvest time, the crops were cut down using wooden sickles with sharp flint blades. The cutting was done by men, while women followed behind, picking up the crops. Irrigation channels were dug to bring water to the fields during the growing season.

This tomb-model shows a coffin being transported on a funerary boat

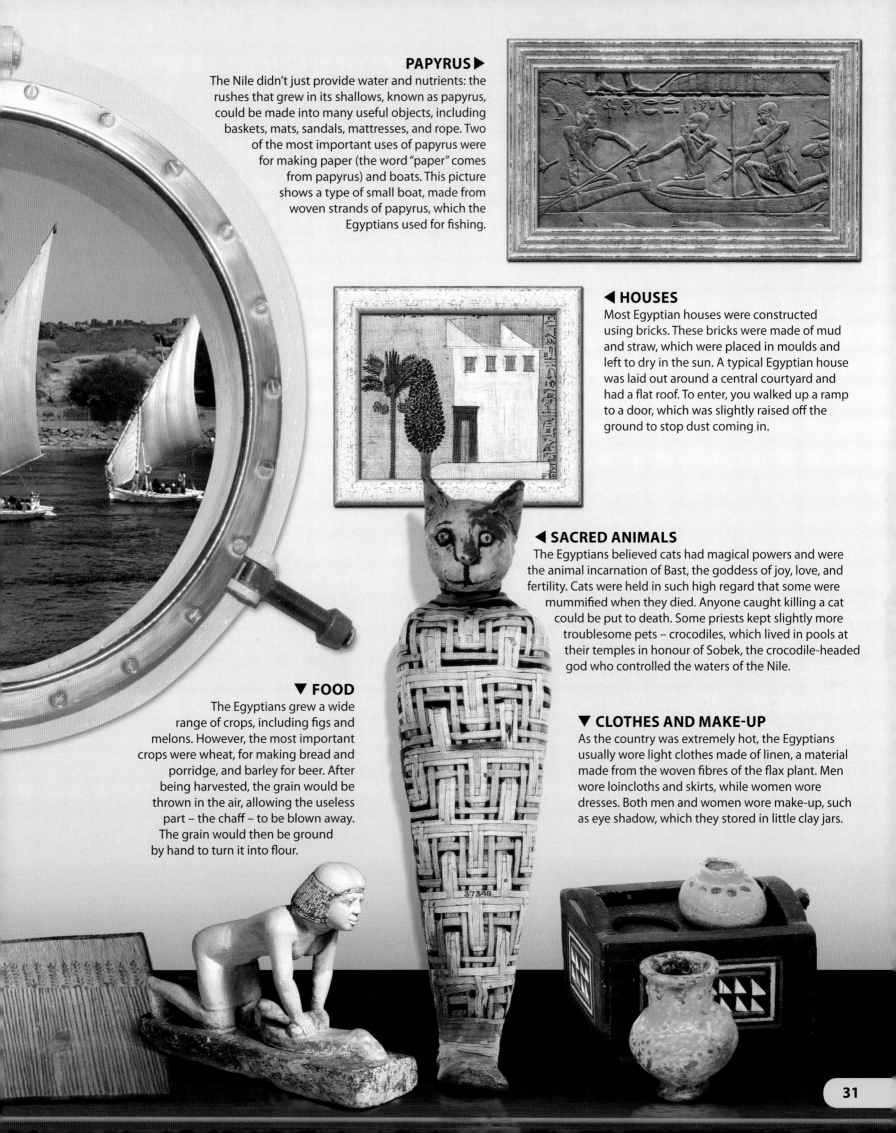

PAPYRUS ▶

The Nile didn't just provide water and nutrients: the rushes that grew in its shallows, known as papyrus, could be made into many useful objects, including baskets, mats, sandals, mattresses, and rope. Two of the most important uses of papyrus were for making paper (the word "paper" comes from papyrus) and boats. This picture shows a type of small boat, made from woven strands of papyrus, which the Egyptians used for fishing.

◀ HOUSES

Most Egyptian houses were constructed using bricks. These bricks were made of mud and straw, which were placed in moulds and left to dry in the sun. A typical Egyptian house was laid out around a central courtyard and had a flat roof. To enter, you walked up a ramp to a door, which was slightly raised off the ground to stop dust coming in.

◀ SACRED ANIMALS

The Egyptians believed cats had magical powers and were the animal incarnation of Bast, the goddess of joy, love, and fertility. Cats were held in such high regard that some were mummified when they died. Anyone caught killing a cat could be put to death. Some priests kept slightly more troublesome pets – crocodiles, which lived in pools at their temples in honour of Sobek, the crocodile-headed god who controlled the waters of the Nile.

▼ FOOD

The Egyptians grew a wide range of crops, including figs and melons. However, the most important crops were wheat, for making bread and porridge, and barley for beer. After being harvested, the grain would be thrown in the air, allowing the useless part – the chaff – to be blown away. The grain would then be ground by hand to turn it into flour.

▼ CLOTHES AND MAKE-UP

As the country was extremely hot, the Egyptians usually wore light clothes made of linen, a material made from the woven fibres of the flax plant. Men wore loincloths and skirts, while women wore dresses. Both men and women wore make-up, such as eye shadow, which they stored in little clay jars.

GODS OF EGYPT

The Egyptians worshipped more than 2,000 gods and goddesses. Each deity had its own distinct responsibilities – there was a god of the Sun, a god of war, and a god of music, for example – and their own unique characteristics. Many were shown with human bodies and animal heads, which made them easy for people to recognize. Offerings were made to the gods to make sure that they looked after the Egyptians, both in this world and in the afterlife.

▲ **Divinity of pharaohs** The pharaoh was not just the most powerful person in Egypt, he was also the chief priest. Pharaohs were considered to be half-man, half-god. The picture above shows the pharaoh Ramses III with the goddess Isis.

▲ **Temples** Every city had a temple, such as this one dedicated to Amun-Ra at Karnak. Only the pharaoh and his priests were allowed in the inner temple where the statue of the god was situated. Grain was stored in the temple, and schooling took place there.

▲ **Rituals** One of the most important religious rituals was the daily "Offering Ceremony". The pharaoh and his priests would dress the statue of the god and offer it food. The god would eat the "essence" of the food; then the priests would eat the real thing.

▲ **Hieroglyphics** The Egyptians developed a form of writing called hieroglyphics. Hieroglyphics used pictures to represent objects, actions, and thoughts. Hieroglyphics were used mainly for religious inscriptions – "hieroglyph" means "sacred writing".

▲ **Rosetta Stone** Egyptian hieroglyphics were deciphered when a stone was discovered in the Egyptian town of Rosetta in 1799. The same piece of text had been engraved on the stone in Greek, Egyptian Demotic, and Hieroglyphics.

▲ **Ra** The creator of all life, Ra was the father of the gods and the god of the Sun. He was believed to accompany the Sun across the sky every day in a boat. He is usually shown, as here, with the head of a hawk and wearing a Sun disk.

▲ **Osiris** Dressed in white and carrying a crook and a flail, Osiris was the ruler of the land of the dead. He was believed to have been murdered by his brother Set, and brought back to life by his wife Isis, who reassembled his body parts.

▲ **Isis** The goddess of fertility, motherhood, and magic, Isis was the sister (and wife) of Osiris. In early Egyptian times, she was portrayed with a throne-shaped crown, but this changed to a cow-horn headdress holding the Sun.

▲ **Anubis** The god of embalming, Anubis is shown here tending to the mummy of a pharaoh. Normally depicted with the head of a jackal, his job was to prepare the dead for their journey into the afterlife. Anubis was the son of Osiris.

▲ **Set** With a head in the shape of a mythical creature called a typhon, Set was the god of chaos, darkness, and storms. He caused trouble with the other gods, killing his younger brother Osiris and poking out the eye of Horus.

▲ **Horus** The pharaoh was regarded as the physical manifestation of the god Horus. Horus was shown with the head of a falcon and wearing the double crown, which symbolized the union of Upper and Lower Egypt.

▲ **Maat** Depicted with wings, Maat was the goddess of truth and harmony. The concept of *maat* – order and justice – was important. The Egyptians tried to be fair and just, so that their hearts would be light enough for them to reach the afterlife.

▶ **Thoth** Shown here on the left with the head of an Ibis, Thoth was the god of wisdom. The Egyptians thought of Thoth as the heart of the creator god Ra, for they believed that the mind lay in the heart. Thoth was often asked to settle disputes between the gods.

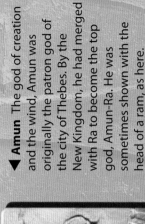

▼ **Amun** The god of creation and the wind, Amun was originally the patron god of the city of Thebes. By the New Kingdom, he had merged with Ra to become the top god, Amun-Ra. He was sometimes shown with the head of a ram, as here.

Anubis, the god of mummification, weighs a soul

THE AFTERLIFE

The Egyptians believed there was an afterlife, but they thought that only some people got to experience it. You had to live your life in the right way, by being good and not committing any crimes. Everything you did counted for or against you in a final reckoning. The Egyptians went to great lengths to prepare their dead for the afterlife and to ensure that their life there was as comfortable as possible.

❶ Judgement of the heart To pass through to the afterlife you had to fulfil three criteria: you had to have your name written down somewhere; your body had to be preserved as a mummy; and you had to have your soul weighed against a feather by the god Anubis. If there was no sin, it would be as light as the feather, and you would pass.

❷ Pyramids Egypt's poor were buried simply in the sand, but royals could expect something more grand. In the Old Kingdom, the pharaohs were laid to rest in enormous stone pyramids. The biggest, Khufu's Pyramid at Giza, is still the largest stone structure ever built. It contains more than two million stone blocks, each weighing more than two tonnes, and took thousands of workers about 20 years to complete.

Tutankhamun was buried with two daggers, one with a blade made of gold, the other iron

❸ Inside a tomb In later years, large obvious pyramids were abandoned in favour of secret underground tombs to try to foil tomb robbers. Inside a tomb, the dead would be buried with items for use in the afterlife, such as food, furniture, jewellery, games, and weapons. The walls were covered with paintings of scenes from the deceased's life and the journey they would take into the afterlife. The grave goods of pharaohs included "eternal helpers" – model servants to help them in the world beyond.

❹ Tutankhamun A great deal of what we know about the contents of royal tombs comes from the amazing finds recovered from the tomb of Pharaoh Tutankhamun. He ruled for just nine years in the 14th century BCE, but his name went down in history when the British archaeologist Howard Carter discovered his tomb in the 1920s. It is the only pharaoh's tomb ever found that had not been raided by tomb robbers.

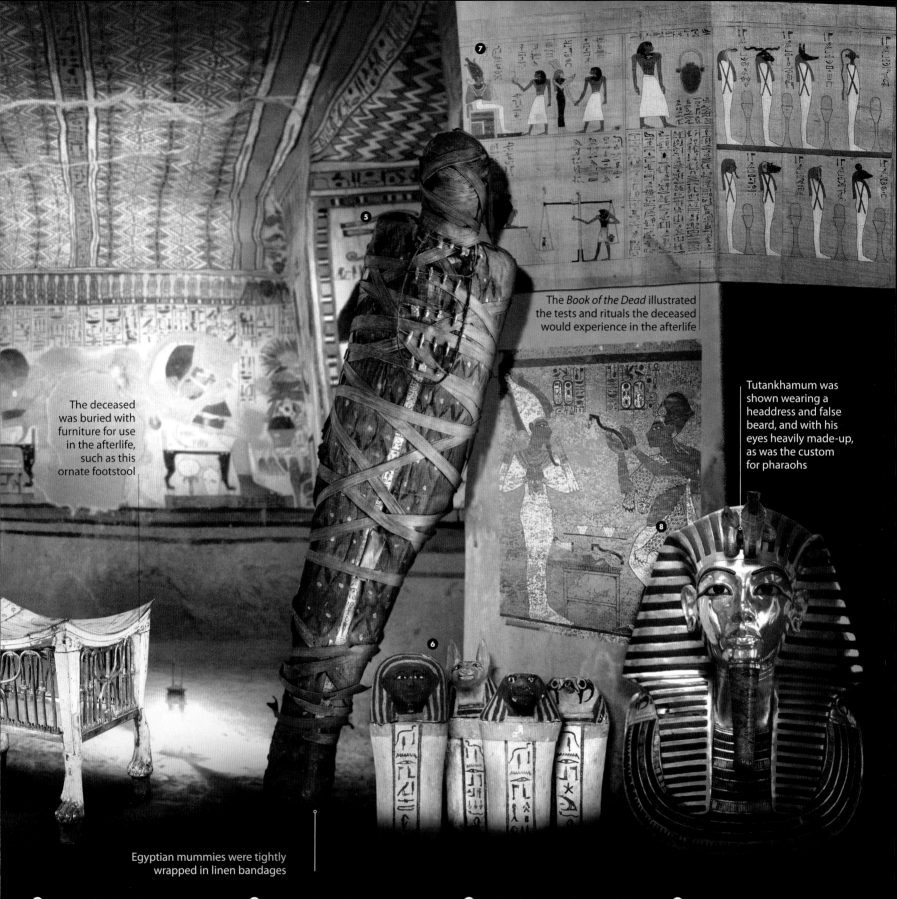

The *Book of the Dead* illustrated the tests and rituals the deceased would experience in the afterlife

The deceased was buried with furniture for use in the afterlife, such as this ornate footstool

Tutankhamum was shown wearing a headdress and false beard, and with his eyes heavily made-up, as was the custom for pharaohs

Egyptian mummies were tightly wrapped in linen bandages

5 Mummification Preserving a body as a mummy took about 70 days. The body was washed and the organs removed. Only the heart was left behind, as the Egyptians believed this was the source of intelligence. The body was dried out using natron, a type of salt, stuffed with linen and sawdust, and wrapped in linen. It was then placed in its coffin ready for the afterlife.

6 Canopic jars The organs removed during mummification were placed in special vessels called canopic jars. The jars had lids in the shape of four gods, each of whom was responsible for a different organ: Imnesty (human head) for the liver, Duamutef (jackal head) for the stomach, Hapy (baboon head) for the lungs, and Qebehsenuf (falcon head) for the intestines.

7 Book of the Dead As one final aid for the afterlife, the deceased would have a copy of the *Book of the Dead* placed inside their coffin. It consisted of various magic spells, songs, stories, and instructions that were written on papyrus. These books were often mass-produced in workshops with spaces left for the individual's name to be added in at a later date.

8 Death masks High-status Egyptians were buried in carved stone coffins called sarcophagi. Inside Tutankhamun's sarcophagus were three gilded wooden coffins, each carved into a likeness of the pharaoh dressed as the god Osiris. In the final coffin lay the mummified body, wearing a death mask of gold, coloured glass, and semi-precious stones.

NUBIA

Around the same time that people were settling down to farming in Egypt, another culture was emerging farther south along the banks of the Nile. This was Nubia, which would become one of Africa's first civilizations. Nubia's history would be closely linked with that of its northern neighbour. In the early years, Egypt was the dominant force, invading Nubia and using it as a source of slaves. Later, the Nubian civilizations would gain the upper hand, ruling Egypt briefly in the first millennium BCE, and even outlasting their more famous rival.

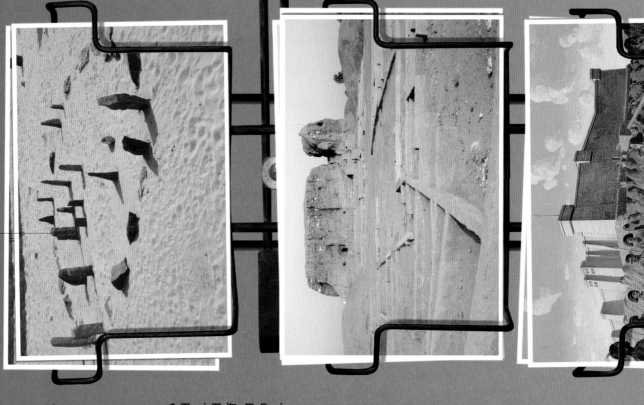

These Nubian megaliths may be one of the world's earliest astronomical devices

▶ EARLY NUBIA

The origins of the Nubian civilization go back to around 5000 BCE, the same time that ancient Egypt was emerging. To begin with, the Nubians were the more advanced people, but Egypt soon overtook them and by the time of the Old Kingdom (2649–2134 BCE) had begun exploiting Nubia for ivory, gold, and slaves. The first Nubian kingdom didn't emerge until after the fall of the Old Kingdom.

▶ KERMA

Nubia's first kingdom was centred on the city of Kerma. This picture shows the remains of one of its giant mud-brick temples. Egypt revived during the Middle Kingdom (2055–1650 BCE) and conquered the northern half of the Kerma kingdom, known as Lower Nubia. At the end of the Middle Kingdom, the Hyksos people from the Middle East invaded Egypt, prompting the Nubians to revolt and retake control of Lower Nubia.

▶ TRADE

Egypt and Kerma may have regularly gone to war, but for most of the time their relationship was based on trade, not conflict. With links to the tropical cultures of Eritrea and Ethiopia, Kerma lay at the heart of a great trading network. Kerma supplied Egypt with a vast range of exotic goods, including gold, copper, ivory, ebony, incense, aromatic oils, and animal skins. All of this trade took place along the Nile.

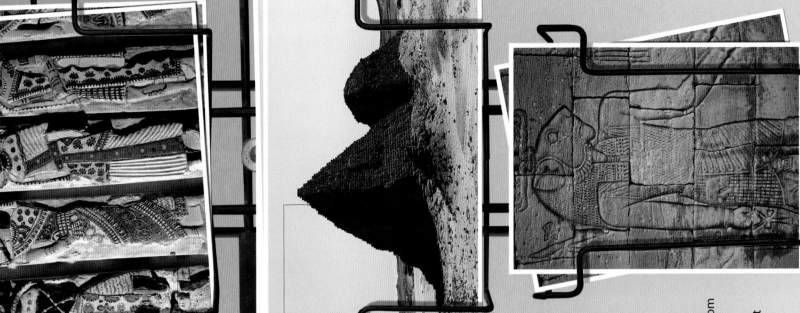

▶ EGYPTIAN RESURGENCE

The Nubian revival was brought to an end by Egypt's resurgence during the New Kingdom (1532–1070 BCE). Pharaoh Tuthmosis I invaded Nubia, sacking Kerma. Later, Ramses II built a giant monument at Abu Simbel in Lower Nubia as a display of Egyptian power over Nubia. However, the Egyptians once again lost control of Nubia at the end of the New Kingdom.

A tile from Abu Simbel showing Nubian prisoners

▶ KUSH

Like the early ancient Egyptians, the Nubians of Kush buried their royals in pyramids

In the first millennium BCE, a new Nubian kingdom, known as Kush, emerged around the city of Napata, to the south of Kerma. As Egypt weakened, so Kush became stronger, and in 712 BCE it conquered Egypt and ruled as its 25th Dynasty. Nubian culture was highly influenced by Egypt at this time. The Nubians worshipped many of the same gods, used Egyptian hieroglyphs, and mummified their dead.

▶ MEROE

The Nubians were expelled from Egypt less than a century after their conquest. In 593 BCE, it was the Egyptians' turn to invade once again. They sacked Napata, forcing the Nubians to move their capital even farther south to Meroe. Here, away from Egyptian influence, a more Nubian culture emerged. They developed their own alphabet and worshipped their own gods, such as Apademak, the lion-headed god (shown here).

▼ AXUM

King Ezana's Stele is 21 m (70 ft) tall

Meroe became a powerful centre of trade in the late first millennium BCE, when it launched raids deep into Egypt. However, it went into decline from around 200 CE onwards and eventually collapsed in 350 CE following an attack by the southern kingdom of Axum in present-day Ethiopia. The kings of Axum marked their burial sites not with pyramids but with giant obelisks, such King Ezana's Stele (shown here).

CARTHAGE

In the eighth century BCE, the Phoenicians founded the city of Carthage on the North African coast. It grew to dominate the Mediterranean trade routes, becoming the richest Phoenician city and, from the sixth century BCE onwards, it started to create its own empire. However, its position came under increasing threat following the rise of Rome in the third century BCE. This clash between two cultures led to a series of wars and the ultimate defeat of Carthage.

▼ THE FIRST PUNIC WAR

As Rome's ambitions grew, it came increasingly into conflict with Carthage. Eventually, war erupted over control of Sicily. This was known as the First Punic War. Fighting began in 264 BCE and, after more than 20 years of intermittent warfare, including the major naval Battle of Mylae (shown here), Rome emerged victorious in 241 BCE. The Romans went on to capture Corsica and Sardinia.

▼ THE CARTHAGINIAN EMPIRE

Carthage was the Mediterranean's major power for a short period of time. Its empire stretched across North Africa and took in parts of southern Spain, as well as the islands of Corsica, Sardinia, and western Sicily. In the sixth century BCE, a new regional rival emerged in Italy – Rome. Relations between the two powers were peaceful to begin with. They even signed a treaty of friendship in 509 BCE.

Spain

Corsica

Rome

Sardinia

Carthage

Sicily

▶ CARTHAGINIAN LEADER

Hannibal (248–183 BCE) became a general when he was just 26. He spent most of his adult life fighting Rome. Following Carthage's defeat in the Second Punic War, Hannibal roamed around the Mediterranean, often joining forces with the enemies of Rome. The Romans kept pursuing him and, rather than face capture, Hannibal took his own life at the age of 64.

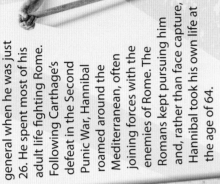

▲ DIDO AND AENEAS

In later centuries, the Punic Wars were turned into legend by the poet Virgil. He told how Dido, the founding queen of Carthage, fell in love with Aeneas. However, Aeneas left Dido and travelled to Italy where his descendants founded Rome. Heartbroken, Dido killed herself and placed a curse on the people of Carthage and Italy, thus ultimately causing the Punic Wars.

▼ SECOND PUNIC WAR

Following its defeat in the First Punic War, Carthage turned its attention to Spain. Unfortunately, Spain was also of growing interest to Rome, and this resulted in the Second Punic War. The Carthaginian general Hannibal led his army, including elephants, over the Alps into Italy to threaten Rome itself. But the Romans managed to halt his progress and Carthage was forced to accept defeat in 201 BCE.

▲ THIRD PUNIC WAR

Carthage's eventual recovery in the second century BCE did not make the Romans happy. In 149 BCE, Roman troops laid siege to the city, eventually defeating it in 146 BCE. The Romans made sure that this defeat would last. They destroyed the city and sold its remaining people into slavery. It was re-founded by Julius Caesar around 100 years later and became a colony for Rome's veteran soldiers.

GREAT ZIMBABWE

South of the Sahara Desert, most of Africa was too hot, too wet, or too full of dangerous insects to support farming. Eventually, civilizations did emerge in the few pockets of land where conditions were favourable, long after the first civilizations of North Africa. The greatest of these was founded by the Shona people on the Zimbabwe Plateau. Here, a great city emerged, built on the proceeds of cattle-rearing and gold-trading.

▼ LAND OF THE FLIES
One of the major difficulties facing sub-Saharan settlement was the presence of swarms of tsetse flies in lowland areas. These large, black insects carried a deadly disease known as sleeping sickness, which could affect both people and cattle. However, in the fifth century CE, the Shona people discovered a plateau set above 1,000 m (3,300 ft), without any flies. Here, they settled to farm, raise cattle, and build their stone settlements.

▼ THE CONICAL TOWER
One of the final structures built in Great Zimbabwe was a huge conical tower. Made of small, shaped stones, the tower is completely solid and stands 10 m (33 ft) high. Archaeologists are unsure what its precise purpose was, but many believe it had some religious significance. Its shape suggests it may have been a symbolic grain bin, representing good harvests.

Tsetse flies feed off the blood of humans and animals

The walls of the Great Enclosure are 250 m (830 ft) long, up to 11 m (37 ft) tall, and 5 m (17 ft) thick

▼ CITY OF STONE

Great Zimbabwe reached its peak from 1200 CE onwards. Over the next couple of centuries, a number of giant stone structures were built – Zimbabwe means "house of stone" in the Shona language. The greatest of these was the Great Enclosure, the largest ancient stone structure south of the Sahara, which may have been the residence of the city's royal family. At its height, the city may have been home to 18,000 people.

▶ ZIMBABWE BIRDS

Sculpted soapstone eagles known as "Zimbabwe Birds" once guarded the top of many of Great Zimbabwe's monuments. The sculptures probably represented the bateleur eagle, which held great religious significance to the Shona people, who believed it to be a messenger of the gods. Today, the bird is the national emblem of Zimbabwe and is featured on the country's flag, banknotes, and coins.

▼ COLLAPSE

Having thrived for several hundred years, Great Zimbabwe's civilization mysteriously collapsed in around 1450 CE. Various possible reasons have been put forward for its decline, including climate change, water shortages, and overgrazing. Whatever the reasons, Great Zimbabwe's trading network was broken up and the city had been entirely abandoned by 1500 CE and was left to fall into ruin (see below).

▼ TRADE

The wealth needed to create Great Zimbabwe was built up largely from trade. The city lay at the centre of a wide-ranging cattle-trading network, and had close ties with the East African civilization of Kilwa. From here, precious local resources, such as gold (shown here), elephant ivory, and animal skins, were exported to far-flung destinations, such as the Middle East and even China. They were exchanged for goods such as pottery and jewellery.

ROMAN MOSAIC
The floors of Roman buildings were often decorated with intricate mosaics, such as this one depicting street musicians. It was found in a villa in Pompeii, a city destroyed by a volcano in 79 CE.

Europe

NEOLITHIC AND BRONZE AGE EUROPE

Although the end of the last ice age saw the beginning of farming in the Middle East, the people of Europe remained hunter-gatherers. Eventually, knowledge of agriculture reached the continent, and by 4000 BCE most of Europe was growing crops. While these early farmers used stone implements, tools and weapons became increasingly sophisticated: first following the introduction of bronze in around 2500 BCE, and then with the adoption of iron from around 1200 BCE.

Some of the stones are 4 m (13 ft) tall and weigh more than 25 tonnes

❶ MEGALITHS

Farming led to the emergence of settled communities and more advanced cultures. Pottery started being made, and in Western Europe people began erecting tombs and temples using large stones called megaliths. One of the most impressive of these is Stonehenge, a circle of enormous stones erected in southwest England around 2500 BCE. How the stones were transported over hundreds of kilometres to the site and put in position is a mystery.

❷ BRONZE AGE

Europe's use of bronze began in Unetice in Poland around 2500 BCE. The technology gradually spread out across the continent, reaching Greece and Italy by around 2300 BCE, Britain and Spain by 2000 BCE, and Scandinavia by 1500 BCE. Cups (such as this one), weapons, tools, and jewellery were among the first bronze items to be made.

❸ CHIEFDOMS

European tribes were led by chiefs who were often buried beneath large earth mounds known as barrows, such as this one in England dating back to around 500 BCE. The barrows' great size, rising above the Bronze Age landscape, as well the amount of time and labour it took to create them, highlighted the chief's status.

❹ ARTS & CRAFTS

The need for chiefs to show their high status in life, as well as in death, led to the development of craftsmanship, particularly metalworking skills. The second millennium BCE saw increased production of finely crafted objects, such as jewellery, tableware, and weapons in gold, bronze, and silver. This picture shows the Nebra Sky Disk, a bronze and gold plate covered in pictures of the Sun, Moon, and stars. It was found in Germany and dates to around 1600 BCE.

❺ TRADE

The increased use of metals in the second millennium BCE, for both military and craft purposes, greatly stimulated the growth of long-distance trade across Europe. Raw materials, such as metal ores, were not evenly distributed across the continent. They often had to be brought long distances to where they were needed. It is probably no coincidence that this period also saw the introduction of wheeled vehicles to Europe. This model of a horse pulling a disc dates from 1400 BCE and is one of the earliest European depictions of a wheeled vehicle.

❻ URNFIELD CULTURE

During the Bronze Age, Europe's population increased dramatically, as improvements in farming techniques and social organization allowed the tribes to produce more food. By the 14th century BCE, a distinct culture had began to dominate Central Europe. It was named the Urnfield Culture after the people's practice of cremating their dead and burying the ashes in pottery urns. The Urnfield people created mass cemeteries that sometimes contained thousands of urns.

❼ THE IRON AGE

The Bronze Age began to come to an end between 1200–1000 BCE following the introduction of a new and even more useful metal – iron. Iron could be used to make extremely sharp weapons and long-lasting tools. The use of iron had spread to Central Europe by 750 BCE and was one of the major reasons behind the rise of the Hallstatt Celts, the successors to the Urnfield Culture.

The Nebra Sky Disk is thought to have been an astronomical instrument

Iron hook used for cutting crops

The handle is made from deer antler

Bronze cup from the 9th century BCE used by the people of the Urnfield Culture

British iron dagger dating from the first millennium BCE

The disk is thought to represent the Sun

MINOANS AND MYCENAEANS

The mountainous island of Crete off Greece's southern coast provided the setting for Europe's first civilization, which emerged in around 2000 BCE. The people who founded this civilization are known as the Minoans after King Minos, a legendary ruler. The kingdoms they created lasted for hundreds of years, despite several natural disasters, before being taken over by the Mycenaeans. Eventually, the Mycenaean civilization was destroyed by a mysterious enemy.

LABYRINTHS AND MINOTAURS ▼

The Minoans built huge palaces, and they also believed bulls were sacred animals. These things combined to create the myth of the Minotaur. This half-man, half-bull monster was trapped inside an impenetrable maze known as the Labyrinth.

Fresco showing dolphins, from the palace at Knossos

◀ TRADE AND PALACES

Crete's mountainous interior was not suited to the type of flood-plain agriculture used in Mesopotamia and Egypt. Instead, the Minoans used the island's slopes to grow crops, such as olives and grapes. These could be turned into portable goods, such as olive oil and wine, and then traded across the Mediterranean. Minoan society was divided into kingdoms, which were ruled from palaces built with the proceeds of this trade, the largest of which was at Knossos.

According to legend, the Minotaur terrorized the people of Crete until it was killed by the hero Theseus

◀ NATURAL DISASTERS

In 1700 BCE, many Minoan palaces were destroyed, possibly by an earthquake. They were rebuilt, but only the palace at Knossos regained its former glory. In 1628 BCE, a volcanic eruption destroyed the Minoan island colony of Akrotiri. The island's palaces were destroyed again in 1450 BCE, but this time as a result of the Mycenaean conquest.

These jars, once used to store Minoan wine and oil, were buried and preserved by the volcanic eruption that destroyed Akrotiri

◀ MYCENAEAN CITADELS

The Mycenaeans emerged on mainland Greece in around 1650 BCE. Their small kingdoms were ruled by kings, who resided in fortified palaces known as citadels. The leading kingdom was ruled from the hilltop citadel of Mycenae itself. The Mycenaeans had much in common with the later Greek culture and worshipped many of the same gods, including Zeus and Apollo.

Mask that may have belonged to the Mycenaean king Agamemnon

▶ WRITING

Both the Minoans and the Mycenaeans developed their own forms of writing, which they inscribed on clay tablets. Minoan writing, known as Linear A, has never been deciphered. For many years no one could read the Mycenaean writing system, called Linear B (shown here), either. However, in the 20th century, scholars finally cracked the code, discovering that the Mycenaeans used a form of language that was similar to ancient Greek.

▼ WAR AND TRADE

The Mycenaeans were a warlike people. In the 15th century BCE, they took over Crete and led raids against Egypt and the Hittite empire. The Mycenaeans also traded widely with other cultures, as the discovery of the *Uluburun*, a 14th-century-BCE Mycenaean shipwreck, showed. On board the wreck were goods from Egypt, sub-Saharan Africa, Canaan, and Assyria.

▼ MYSTERIOUS DEMISE

Unfortunately, the translation of Linear B did not reveal the reasons for the collapse of Mycenaean civilization in around 1200 BCE. It is clear that Mycenae's cities were attacked and destroyed, but no one knows by whom. Some historians believe it was the "Sea Peoples", a little understood group of warlike migrants. Following Mycenae's decline, Greece entered a 400-year "Dark Age" when its culture declined and writing fell out of use.

Replica of the wooden horse with which the Mycenaeans tricked their way to victory in the Trojan War

▶ THE TROJAN WAR

One of the best known Greek myths tells the story of a war between the Mycenaeans and the Trojans. After 10 years of fighting, the Mycenaeans won by smuggling soldiers hidden inside a giant wooden horse into Troy. The tale was probably based on a real battle in the 13th century BCE. It was kept alive by word of mouth during the Dark Age, before being written down.

This is a carving of the Philistines, possible descendants of the "Sea Peoples"

GREEK CITY-STATES

From the eighth century BCE, Greece began to emerge from the four-century-long cultural decline, known as the "Dark Age", which had been prompted by the fall of Mycenae. On the mainland, individual settlements, often separated from each other by the country's many mountains, grew into strong, independent city-states. Athens, Sparta, and Corinth were the most powerful of these cities, often going to war for control of the Greek world. Between them, they helped to develop a thriving and hugely influential civilization.

▶ ATHENS

Filled with fine buildings and named after the Greek goddess Athena, Athens was the largest and most influential of the Greek city-states. Throughout its history it was involved in numerous wars, including conflicts with the Persians in the early fifth century BCE, but it was also a great centre of learning. Its port, known as the Piraeus, was home to Greece's largest navy.

An enormous statue of Athena stood inside Athens's Parthenon

▼ SPARTA

This helmet once belonged to a soldier from Sparta, Athens's great rival. In order to achieve military superiority over its rival cities, Sparta became obsessed with preparing its citizens for war. All male Spartan citizens had to serve in the army, beginning their training at the age of seven. Boys were taken away from their families and taught combat skills, pain tolerance, and dedication to the Spartan state.

▼ THE ACROPOLIS

Early Athens was a defended settlement on a hill known as the Acropolis. As Athens became more successful, the people moved down the hill and the Acropolis became the most sacred part of the city. Between 447 and 432 BCE, a temple – the Parthenon – dedicated to Athena, was built on its highest point.

▼ DEMOCRACY

Early Greek states were run by kings. Over time, however, more people wanted to be involved in the decision-making process. The kings were overthrown and new forms of government adopted. The most radical was in Athens where every freeborn Athenian man over 20 could vote on all decisions. This system was called "democracy", which means "people's power".

Public votes were held at a vast meeting called an Assembly

▶ GREEK TRADE AND CRAFTS

The Greeks traded widely in oil, wine, pottery, and metal work. The success of this trade inspired the growth of the craft industry. Every town had a potters' quarter, where ceramics were produced in vast quantities, decorated with pictures of gods, heroes, and myths, as well as scenes of everyday life. Early pots featured black figures on a red background, as on the pot on the right. However, from the fifth century BCE onwards, this style was reversed to show red figures on a black background, as on the pot on the left.

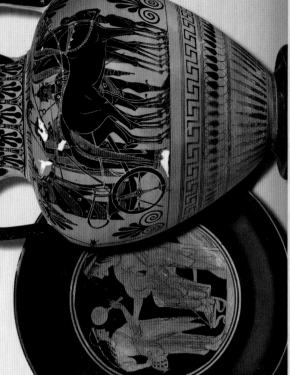

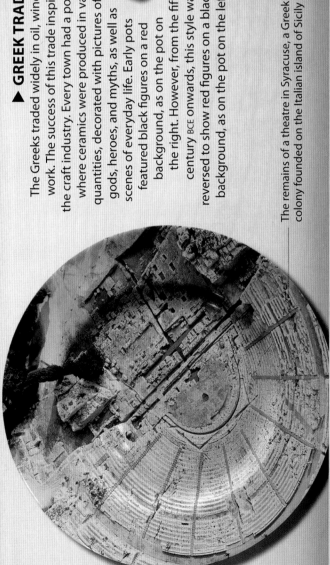

The remains of a theatre in Syracuse, a Greek colony founded on the Italian island of Sicily

▲ GREEK EXPANSION

As prosperity increased and populations swelled, the Greek cities began to outgrow their resources. The city governments decided to send citizens abroad to establish new colonies. The colonists were chosen by lot and anyone who refused to go was punished. New colonies were founded in Turkey, Sicily, Italy, and even as far west as France, resulting in the spread of Greek civilization throughout much of the Mediterranean.

▼ ARMOUR AND WEAPONS

This plate is decorated with an image of a Greek infantry soldier, known as a hoplite. Hoplites protected themselves with bronze helmets, made-to-measure breastplates, shields, and leg guards called greaves. Their main weapon was a long spear. Soldiers had to buy all their own equipment, so only men from wealthy families could afford to be hoplites.

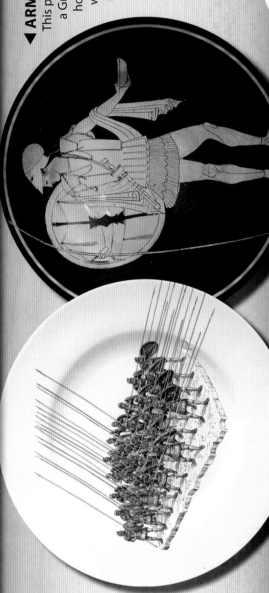

GREEK STYLE OF WAR ▲

The Greeks were great military innovators. They invented the phalanx, an infantry formation where the soldiers lined up in a rectangle with locked shields and spears poking forwards. They were assisted by groups of archers and stone-slingers. From the fourth century BCE, the Greeks devised a range of large weapons, including catapults, flame-throwers, and battering rams, for laying siege to cities.

▶ TRIREMES

The Greeks also fought at sea using long ships known as triremes powered by three lines of rowers, set one above the other. Each trireme had 170 rowers and a pointed metal ram at the front for sinking enemy ships. There was also a sail and a magic eye painted at the front to help guide them. At its peak, Athens had a force of about 300 triremes.

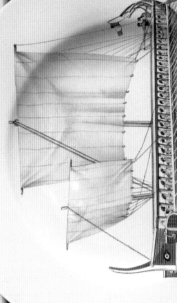

THE GREEK WORLD

Life in ancient Greece was very different depending on whether you were a man or a woman, rich or poor, free or a slave. Men owned most of the property, served in the army, and oversaw the production of crops. Women stayed at home, looked after the children, and supervised the slaves. Some slaves were captives from battles, some were the children of slaves, while others were poor people who had been sold into slavery by their families.

3 WOMEN IN ANCIENT GREECE

A woman had few rights in ancient Greece and was regarded as the property of men – first of her father and then of her husband. Girls did not go to school, but stayed at home and were taught to weave, make clothes, and cook. Occasionally, girls from wealthy families were taught how to read. This is a sculpture of Sappho, one of the few female poets in ancient Greece.

7 GREEK CLOTHES

Most Greek clothes were made of wool, although linen was also used. The main garment for both men and women was a type of tunic, known as a *chiton*. It consisted of two large rectangles of cloth fastened together with brooches or pins and gathered at the waist with a belt. In cold weather, people could also wear a cloak, known as a *himation*, over the top of this.

1 GODS AND GODDESSES

The Greeks believed their world was controlled by various gods who lived on Mount Olympus, the highest point in Greece. These gods looked and behaved much like humans: they fell in love, fought, and had children. Each god had its own area of expertise – for example, hunting, grain growing, love, and war. The Greeks honoured their gods with temples and sacrifices of food and animals.

4 DEATH AND AFTERLIFE

When somebody died, the Greeks believed they went to an underground world called Hades. This is why the dead were buried in the ground. After death, the deceased would have to pay a ferryman to transport them across the River Styx to the kingdom of the dead, as is being shown in this picture. The family would leave a coin with the corpse for the journey.

2 FESTIVALS AND GAMES

Athletic festivals, such as the Olympic Games, were held to honour the gods. Athletes competed in many of the same sports as at the modern Olympics, including long jump and running races, as shown on this vase from the fifth century BCE. Unlike the modern games, however, the competitors were naked. The Olympic Games were held for more than 1,000 years, from 776 BCE until 393 CE in the Roman era.

5 THE TREASURY

Athenians kept their money in a treasury. This treasury was built at Delphi in central Greece in honour of Apollo, the god of prophecy. Apollo was believed to make predictions about the future through his priestess, the oracle. The cities kept their treasuries at Delphi because they knew that no other Greeks would dare plunder them for fear of offending Apollo.

6 THE GREEK HOME

Greek homes were usually made of sun-dried bricks, topped with clay-tile roofs, and painted white. They were built around a central courtyard and had just a few windows (without glass). Other features included a hearth for cooking, a dining room, and an entrance porch. All of the housework was carried out by a team of slaves.

8 FOOD AND DRINK

The Greeks' daily staples were bread, made from wheat, and porridge, made from barley. They also ate a range of vegetables, including peas, olives, onions, garlic, and cabbage. Their main sources of protein were cheese (most families kept a goat) and fish. Meat was usually eaten only at religious festivals. The Greeks drank wine, usually mixed with water.

Columns at entrance to Athenian treasury

Entrance porch

This terracotta figurine shows a woman wearing a himation and carrying a fan

Drinking cup

Athena was the Greek goddess of wisdom and warfare

GREEK INNOVATORS

The Greeks developed an entirely new way of thinking about the world called "philosophy", which means "love of wisdom". Greek philosophers spent a lot of time studying and debating the mysteries of the Universe, trying to figure out how the world worked, and how people should behave. Other Greek thinkers made great advances in the fields of theatre, literature, science, mathematics, and medicine. These would have profound effects on the development of Western history.

▼ THEATRE

The Greeks invented the concept of the theatre play. The first plays were simple dramas held in honour of the wine god, Dionysus. Over time, these plays became more sophisticated and were very popular. Soon every town in the Greek world had an open-air theatre, usually cut into the side of a hill. These theatres could seat up to 15,000 people. Theatrical competitions were even held between the city states. Many Greek theatres survive to this day.

PHILOSOPHY – SOCRATES ▼

The Athenian Socrates (c. 469– 399 BCE) was one of the most famous and influential of all Greek philosophers. He encouraged his students to question everything and to explore ideas through discussion and debate. However, the Athenian authorities grew irritated by Socrates's constant questioning. He was accused of disrespecting the gods, found guilty, and was forced to commit suicide by taking poison. He left no written works behind.

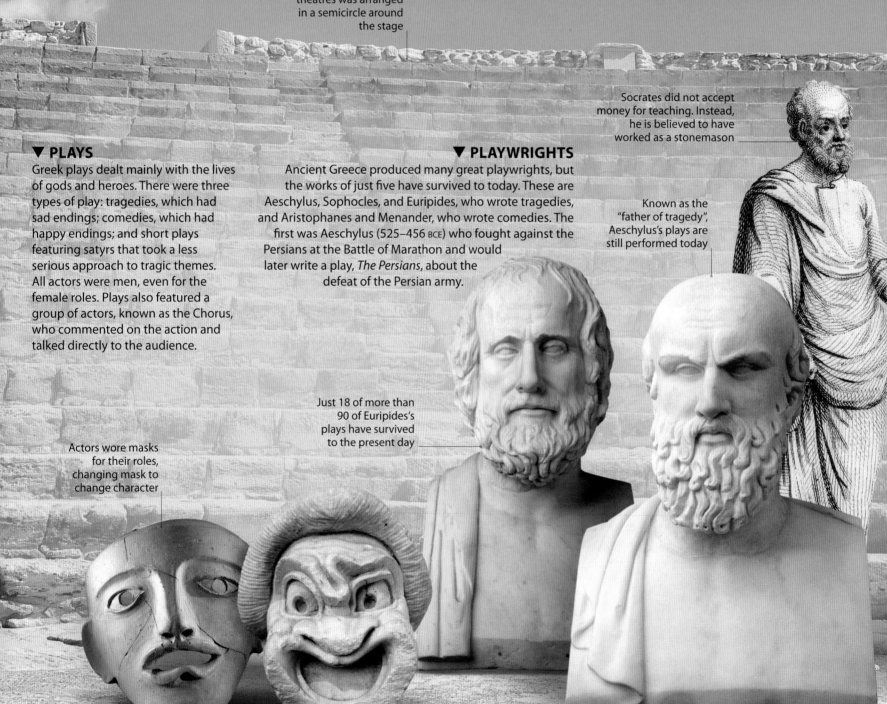

The seating in Greek theatres was arranged in a semicircle around the stage

Socrates did not accept money for teaching. Instead, he is believed to have worked as a stonemason

▼ PLAYS

Greek plays dealt mainly with the lives of gods and heroes. There were three types of play: tragedies, which had sad endings; comedies, which had happy endings; and short plays featuring satyrs that took a less serious approach to tragic themes. All actors were men, even for the female roles. Plays also featured a group of actors, known as the Chorus, who commented on the action and talked directly to the audience.

▼ PLAYWRIGHTS

Ancient Greece produced many great playwrights, but the works of just five have survived to today. These are Aeschylus, Sophocles, and Euripides, who wrote tragedies, and Aristophanes and Menander, who wrote comedies. The first was Aeschylus (525–456 BCE) who fought against the Persians at the Battle of Marathon and would later write a play, *The Persians*, about the defeat of the Persian army.

Known as the "father of tragedy", Aeschylus's plays are still performed today

Just 18 of more than 90 of Euripides's plays have survived to the present day

Actors wore masks for their roles, changing mask to change character

▼ PHILOSOPHY – PLATO

Most of what we know about Socrates comes from the works of one of his students, Plato (428–348 BCE). Plato was also a great philosopher in his own right. He composed works on a wide range of subjects, including the nature of human understanding, the role of government, and mathematics. He founded the world's first school for philosophers in Athens, known as "The Academy". This school continued operating until 529 CE.

▼ PHILOSOPHY – ARISTOTLE

Plato had his own star pupil, Aristotle (384–322 BCE), who would become one of the most respected of all Greek thinkers. His influence would be particularly far-reaching because he was the tutor of the young Alexander of Macedon (later Alexander the Great). As he conquered a large area of Asia, Alexander spread the Greek values and the Greek way of life, as taught to him by Aristotle.

▼ MATHS – PYTHAGORAS

Pythagoras (c. 570–495 BCE) was one of the most important figures in the early development of mathematics. He believed that the Universe worked according to mathematical laws. He was also interested in the rules of music – how notes could be used to create tunes out of sound. Pythagoras travelled widely, moving to a Greek colony in southern Italy, where he became the head of a group of leading thinkers known as the Pythagoreans.

"Plato" is a nickname meaning "broad". His real name was Aristocles

Aristotle wrote works on logic, science, poetry, and zoology among other topics

Pythagoras is best known for his theorem about the properties of right-angle triangles: $a^2 + b^2 = c^2$

▼ MEDICINE

When ancient Greeks felt ill, they would pray at the temple of Asclepius, the god of medicine. If cured, the patient might leave a model of the cured body part as an offering. Greek medicine became more sophisticated after the arrival of Hippocrates (c. 460–370 BCE). This Greek physician prescribed physical treatments for illnesses, rather than relying on prayer and magic. He is often called the "father of modern medicine".

Models of cured body parts

ALEXANDER THE GREAT

Alexander was one of the greatest military commanders: he never lost a battle. He was also an important promoter of Greek culture, even though he was not himself Greek. Alexander was from the kingdom of Macedonia to the north of the Greek city-states, but was brought up to have a love of Greek culture. Between 334 BCE and his sudden death in 223 BCE, he conquered the largest empire that had yet existed, spreading Greek culture wherever he went.

▼ CONQUESTS

Alexander's father, Philip of Macedon, conquered the Greek city-states and decided to lead them in an attack against the Persians, then the most powerful force in the Middle East. He was murdered before he could carry out his plans, but Alexander continued with the invasion, conquering Persia, Egypt, and territory stretching all the way from Greece to India.

▼ ALEXANDER'S LEGACY

Alexander had a deep love for Greek culture, inspired by his tutor, the philosopher Aristotle. This made him not just Greece's greatest warrior, but also its leading cultural ambassador. During the course of his campaigns, he founded some 70 cities, many of them called Alexandria, where he introduced Greek literature, religious beliefs, language, money (shown here), medicine, and art.

This coin from the reign of Alexander shows the Greek goddess Athena

▶ ALEXANDRIA

After Alexander's death, his empire was divided between his generals. However, Alexander's cultural revolution continued as the territories he had conquered came under the influence of Greek culture. Alexandria in Egypt (shown here) became one of the largest cities in the ancient world. It had an enormous lighthouse, which was one of the Seven Wonders of the Ancient World.

▶ GREEK ARCHITECTURE

Architecture was one of the most obvious ways in which Greek culture was spread. Wherever they settled in the Middle East and the Mediterranean, the Greeks built cities that were filled with distinctive columned buildings. This picture shows the ruins of a temple in Priene, a city on the west coast of Turkey.

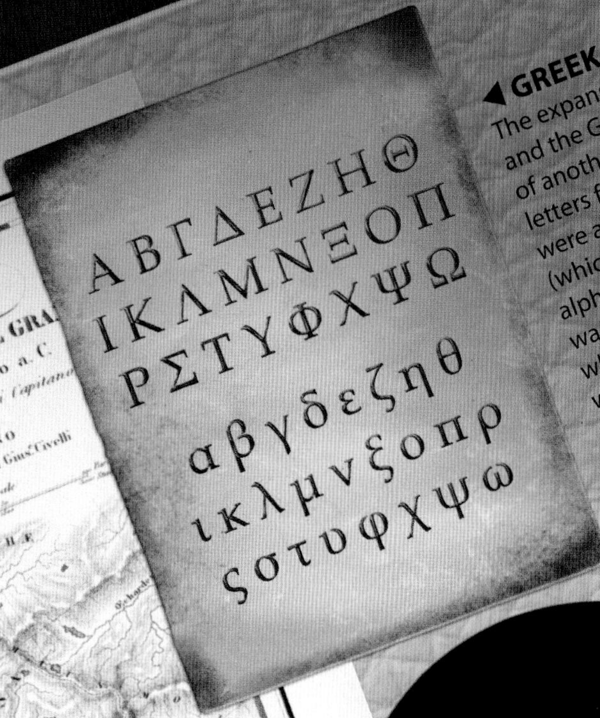

GREEKALPHABET

ΑΒΓΔΕΖΗΘ
ΙΚΛΜΝΞΟΠ
ΡΣΤΥΦΧΨΩ
αβγδεζηθ
ικλμνξοπρ
ςστυφχψω

▶ **GREEKALPHABET**
The expansion of Greek culture and the Greek language helped the spread of another Greek innovation – the use of separate letters for vowels and consonants. Greek letters were adapted from the earlier Phoenician alphabet (which had grown out of the even earlier Canaanite alphabet). The Roman alphabet, which we still use, was ultimately derived from the Greek alphabet, while the Greek alphabet is still used today for writing modern Greek.

IMPERO
D'ALESSANDRO IL GRAN
Dal 405 al 520 a.C.
Per Ferd.º Arrigoni Capitano
MILANO
Stabilimento di Gius.º Civelli

▶ **ROMAN TAKEOVER**
During the second and first centuries BCE, the Hellenistic world was gradually taken over by Rome. Although they were the new masters of the Mediterranean, the Romans were hugely influenced by Greek culture. They adopted much of the Greek religion, language, art, and architecture – as shown by this Greek-style temple in Rome.

RISE OF ROME

In around 1000 BCE, a people known as the Latins migrated to Italy. There they founded Rome, the city-state that would become the continent's dominant power. Initially ruled by a monarch, Rome became a republic in the sixth century BCE, governed by elected officials. This system worked well for a while, helping Rome to expand its territory across Italy and beyond. However, civil war between Rome's leading generals eventually lead to the republic's collapse.

▲ THE ETRUSCANS

Prior to the rise of Rome, the dominant people of Italy were the Etruscans. Etruscan culture was highly advanced. They used an alphabet based on Greek letters, and created ornate artworks, such as this tomb painting. Some of Rome's first kings were Etruscans, but eventually Etruria was taken over by Rome.

▼ ROMULUS AND REMUS

As Rome became more powerful, so its people began to create legends about their past. One of the most popular of these concerned Romulus and Remus, who were the twin sons of Mars, the god of war. Abandoned by their mother, they were brought up by a she-wolf and went on to found Rome in 753 BCE. However, in a quarrel over who should be king, Romulus killed Remus and named the new city after himself.

▶ THE MONARCHY

The early Roman state was ruled by kings with the help of the Senate, an assembly of leading citizens known as senators. As Rome began to expand in the sixth century BCE, so the kings began to act in an increasingly independent way. When King Tarquin the Proud (ruled 535–509 BCE) ignored the advice of the Senate, he was overthrown, and Rome became a republic.

Timeline of Roman history

1000 BCE	First villages in Tiber Valley
753 BCE	Legendary foundation of Rome
509 BCE	Last king is overthrown; Rome becomes a republic
264–146 BCE	Rome defeats Carthage in Punic wars and takes control of North Africa
49 BCE	Julius Caesar is declared dictator of Rome
44 BCE	Julius Caesar is assassinated, leading to civil war
27 BCE	Octavian becomes the first emperor of the Roman empire; changes his name to Augustus
43 CE	Rome invades Britain
79 CE	Vesuvius erupts, destroying Pompeii
98–117 CE	Emperor Trajan builds the empire up to its greatest extent
122–123 CE	Hadrian's Wall is built
391 CE	Christianity becomes official religion in Rome
410 CE	Rome sacked by Alaric and the Goths
476 CE	The Western Roman empire comes to an end
1453 CE	The fall of Constantinople brings the Eastern Roman empire to an end

A statue depicting the she-wolf with the twins, Romulus and Remus

▶ THE REPUBLIC

After the monarchy was overthrown, the Romans decided not to let any one person become too powerful. During the time of the Republic, the Senate elected two people to be Rome's rulers, or consuls, for just one year. However, in times of crisis, a single leader, known as a dictator, could be appointed for six months only. This picture shows Cincinnatus, who was called to become Dictator of Rome while working on his farm.

◀ THE TRIBUNES

As the senators were rich aristocrats (known as patricians) whose appointment was for life, the poor and the wealthy from non-noble families (known as plebs) were excluded from power. This led to revolts in the fifth century BCE. To solve the problem, a new position, called the tribune, was created to represent the views of the plebs. From 342 BCE onwards, one consul was always a pleb. This image shows the tribune Tiberius Gracchus (c. 168–133 BCE).

▲ THE TRIUMVIRATE

The growing power of the generals and the weakness of the state was again shown in 61 BCE when another general, Pompey, clashed with the Senate. He formed a political alliance, known as the Triumvirate, with two other generals, Crassus and Julius Caesar (shown here). The alliance sidelined the Senate. But it did not last long. By 49 BCE, following a brief civil war, Caesar had emerged as the undisputed master of Rome.

Sulla, the Dictator of Rome

▲ ROMAN EXPANSION

From the fifth century BCE onwards, Rome's power grew and by 200 BCE it was in control of much of the western Mediterranean. In the second century BCE, southern France (Gaul) and Greece were also conquered. But the more territory the Roman state took over, the more it seemed to want. At the height of its power in the early second century CE, it controlled an empire stretching from Britain to the Middle East, as shown in this map.

▲ END OF THE REPUBLIC

Caesar declared himself Dictator for life. He was popular with the common people because he passed laws in their favour. But his reforms were disliked by the senators, and he was assassinated in 44 BCE. This led to another civil war, which was won by Caesar's adopted son, Octavian, at the Battle of Actium in 31 BCE (shown here). Octavian ruled alone, marking the end of the Roman republic and the beginning of the Roman empire.

▶ MARIUS VS SULLA

The creation of professional soldiers by the consul and general Gaius Marius (157–86 BCE) increased the effectiveness of the Roman army. It also made the generals more powerful, leading them into conflict, both with each other and the Senate. In the first century BCE, the armies of Marius and another general, Sulla (138–78 BCE), went to war to decide who would be Rome's top general. Sulla won and was appointed Dictator of Rome, before retiring shortly before his death.

ROMAN EMPIRE

The founding of the Roman empire in 27 BCE marked the beginning of the most successful period in Rome's history. From this point on, Rome was no longer ruled by elected officials but by an emperor. In the early years of empire, most emperors were the relatives of former emperors. However, as time went on, it became commonplace for generals to seize power, but this led to instability. In the fifth century CE, a combination of internal tensions and foreign threats caused the western half of the Roman empire to collapse.

▲ AUGUSTUS

Following victory over his rivals, Octavian, now known as Augustus ("revered one"), effectively became the Roman empire's monarch. However, knowing the Roman people's distrust of kings, he gave himself the title of *Princeps* instead, meaning "first citizen". His rule lasted until 14 CE and brought much-needed stability to Rome and its territories.

▲ EXPANSION

The empire continued to expand in the first century CE under Augustus's successors. Claudius (ruled 41–54 CE) conquered Britain as far north as Scotland. Later, the Spanish-born Trajan (ruled 98–117 CE) became Rome's first non-Italian emperor. He was also one of its greatest military leaders, taking control of Dacia, Armenia, and Mesopotamia, and building the empire up to the greatest extent in its history. His campaigns are recorded on Trajan's column, which stands in Rome.

▼ CONSTANTINE

The civil war was won by Constantine (ruled 306–337 CE), the first Christian emperor. He abolished the Tetrarchy, ruling alone, and legalized the previously outlawed religion of Christianity. A new capital, Constantinople, was constructed to rule over the eastern half of the empire.

▲ HADRIAN

Trajan's successor Hadrian (ruled 117–138 CE) was concerned with securing the empire's borders. In Britain, the Roman army had been unable to subdue the tribes of northern Britain. Hadrian decided to build a heavily fortified wall to keep out the northern tribes.

▲ MARCUS AURELIUS

During the reign of Marcus Aurelius (ruled 161–180 CE), the empire came under attack from Germanic tribes in the north and the Parthian empire in the east. The situation worsened further under Commodus (ruled 180–192 CE), who was eventually assassinated.

▲ CRISIS

In the third century CE, emperors came and went swiftly, with few lasting more than five years. Most were generals who briefly gained the position by assassinating their predecessor. Maximinus Thrax (ruled 235–238 CE) was the first emperor to begin his career as an enlisted soldier.

▲ DIOCLETIAN

Emperor Diocletian (ruled 284–305 CE) realized the empire was now too big for one man to control. So he divided it into the western and the eastern empires. Each was ruled by an emperor and an assistant in an arrangement known as the Tetrarchy (shown above). It worked well for 20 years before civil war broke out.

◀ THE END IN THE WEST

The empire in the west grew increasingly weak in the fifth century. In 410 CE, Rome was sacked by a Germanic tribe called the Visigoths. Rather than guarding the empire's borders, the generals fought among themselves, allowing foreign invaders to take over. In 476 CE, the last Roman emperor, Romulus Augustulus, was overthrown and the western empire collapsed.

◀ ROME IN THE EAST

The eastern empire continued after the fall of the western half. Now known as the Byzantine empire, it was ruled from Constantinople. At its heart was the Hagia Sophia, the world's largest church. The empire lasted for nearly a thousand years, until Constantinople finally fell to the Muslim Ottoman empire in 1453.

ROMAN CITY LIFE

The Roman empire could be regarded as a giant network of cities. When the Romans conquered a new land, they built towns and cities there for their soldiers and administrators. Pompeii in southern Italy was a typical Roman city, filled with homes, temples, and bathing complexes. We know more about Pompeii than most other Roman cities because many of its buildings were preserved in ash following a volcanic eruption in the first century CE.

▼ ROMAN CITY

Roman cities, such as Pompeii (shown here), were nearly always built with streets laid out in straight lines. Entrance to the city was through a number of gates, such as the Ercolano Gate. At the centre was the forum, an open space where the main market was held. Other buildings included the basilica (town hall), theatres, and baths, such as the Stabian and Forum Baths.

▲ ROMAN HOUSES

In a Roman city, the type of house in which people lived depended on their social status. The poor lived in cramped conditions, while rich plebs and patricians lived in large family homes, such as this one belonging to the mayor of Pompeii. These houses had tiled roofs and large rooms, arranged around a central courtyard, with ornate mosaic floors, as well as toilets, baths, and private temples.

1. Ercolano Gate
2. House of Faun
3. Forum Baths
4. Magistrate fresco
5. Temple of Apollo
6. Basillica

7. Forum
8. Theatres
9. Stabian Baths
10. Mayor's house
11. Amphitheatre

◄ ROMAN RELIGION

The Romans had their own gods, which they worshipped at their city temples, such as Pompeii's Temple of Apollo (shown here). They were also great collectors of other people's religions. For example, they adopted the Persian god of light, Mithras. For many years, the emperors were worshipped as gods, until Constantine became the first emperor to convert to Christianity in the fourth century CE.

◀ ROMAN ART

Every well-to-do city home would be adorned with pieces of art, such as this mosaic from the House of Faun warning people about a guard dog. The Romans were expert mosaic makers, creating intricate pictures using tiny pieces of coloured stone and glass. Frescoes (wall paintings created on wet plaster) were also very popular.

▼ ROMAN CLOTHES

In this Pompeii fresco of a magistrate and his wife, the man is wearing a toga. This was a long piece of woollen cloth, perhaps up to 6 m (20 ft) long, that was wrapped around the body. The toga was a ceremonial form of dress worn only by high-ranking male officials. For day-to-day living, people wore tunics. Women also wore the *stola*, a type of long, pleated dress. Everyone wore leather sandals or boots.

▼ ROMAN GAMES

Pompeii, like most Roman cities, had an amphitheatre where spectator sports were held. These included battles between men and wild animals and gladiatorial contests in which specially trained warriors, known as gladiators, fought each other. The biggest was Rome's Colosseum, which could hold 70,000 spectators. Many larger Roman towns also had a circus for chariot races.

▲ POMPEII

In 79 CE, Mount Vesuvius erupted, covering Pompeii with a thick layer of volcanic ash. The city lay buried and forgotten about until it was rediscovered in 1599. The houses had been remarkably well preserved, and many of the original frescoes and mosaics were still intact.

ROMAN ARMY

The Roman army was one of the most efficient fighting forces in the ancient world. Between the second century BCE and the second century CE, it conquered an empire that stretched across Europe, North Africa, and the Middle East. Unlike the warriors of most other ancient civilizations, Rome's soldiers were full-time professionals. They trained constantly for battle and were rewarded with money and land after victories. However, soldiers who fought poorly were punished severely.

❶ THE ROMAN LEGION

The Roman army was a well-organized force made up of 30 units known as legions. Each legion was made up of 4,000–6,000 infantry soldiers, known as legionaries. A legion was made up of 10 cohorts, while a cohort was made up of six groups of some 80 legionnaries, called centuries. Roman legions usually included 120 horsemen whose main tasks were to act as scouts and as despatch riders.

All Roman soldiers were male, at least 20 years old, and were expected to serve in the army for 25 years. Soldiers shared the spoils of victory, but defeat could lead to a whole legion being disbanded in disgrace.

Each legion carried a flag, known as a *vexillum*, to identify it

❷ EARLY ARMIES

In the early days of Rome, there were strict rules about who could serve in the army. Only citizens who were landowners were allowed to be soldiers and they had to provide their own equipment. These rules were changed at the end of the second century BCE by the consul Gaius Marius, shown here being carried by his troops. He allowed landless citizens to join and made sure that the state provided their equipment.

❸ NON-CITIZEN SOLDIERS

From its earliest days, Rome had often hired non-citizens to fight alongside its armies on a temporary basis. During the rule of the first emperor Augustus, laws were passed allowing non-citizens to serve permanently in the Roman army. Known as auxiliaries, they were paid less than citizen soldiers, but could earn Roman citizenship by performing well in battle. This picture shows an auxiliary wearing an iron chain mail shirt for protection.

❹ WEAPONS

A Roman soldier protected himself with chain mail or armour made of strips of iron and leather, an iron helmet called a *galea*, and a curved rectangular shield known as a *scutum*. He attacked his enemies using two main weapons: a long throwing spear called a *pilum* and a short sword for stabbing called a *gladius*. Most fighting was done on foot and at close quarters.

❺ ROMAN ROADS

The Romans built a great network of roads, connecting the entire empire. The main purpose for these was to help troops move as quickly as possible. Rome's first road, the Appian Way (shown here), was built between Rome and Capua in 312 BCE to hurry soldiers into battle against the Samnites, a rival people in southern Italy. At its peak, the empire had some 400,000 km (250,000 miles) of roads.

❻ TACTICS AND FORMATION

The Romans were inventive fighters, often coming up with new ways of beating their enemies. One of their most effective tactics was called the "tortoise" (*testudo*). For this, a group of soldiers would hold their shields tightly together, both in front and above them, like the shell of a tortoise, so they couldn't be hit by flying missiles. The Romans also used a triangle-shaped formation called the "wedge" to charge at the enemy.

❼ BIG WEAPONS

The Romans also had a range of large weapons that could be used to attack their enemies from a long distance. These included the *ballista*, a giant crossbow, which fired iron-tipped bolts. When attacking a city, soldiers could use an *onager*, a type of giant catapult, capable of flinging 70 kg (150 lb) rocks through walls.

Bolts fired from a ballista could puncture any armour

The "tortoise" formation was often used during sieges

THE ANCIENT CELTS

The Celts emerged in Europe during the first millennium BCE. Made up of different tribes, the people shared technologies, art styles, and beliefs, and they spoke similar languages. But for most of their history, the Celts did not have clearly defined states and they never created a united empire. They enjoyed their greatest period of success between the fifth and first centuries BCE, when they were Western Europe's dominant civilization. After that point, many Celtic tribes were defeated and taken over by the Romans.

❶ ORIGINS

In Europe, from around 1200 BCE onwards, a new culture, called the Hallstatt Culture, developed out of the then dominant Urnfield Culture. The culture is named after Hallstatt, Austria, where some Celts became rich and powerful by mining salt (then a precious commodity) in nearby mountains. This picture shows a bag and shovel used by the salt miners. This culture spread throughout much of Central Europe.

❷ LA TÈNE

After 450 BCE, a new Celtic culture emerged in Germany and France. The La Tène Culture's ornate art style was adopted by Celts across mainland Europe and in Britain and Ireland. This picture shows a highly decorated bronze mirror from Britain, dating back to the first century BCE. At the civilization's peak, Celtic communities could be found all the way from Ireland in the West to Turkey in the East.

❸ TRIBES AND CHIEFS

On occasion, the Celts would unite to fight against a common enemy, such as Rome, but most of the time the tribes remained independent of each other. Each tribe was headed by a chieftain who oversaw the farming and production of craft goods, and led the tribe in times of war. Over the centuries, the Celtic tribes became increasingly sophisticated. They founded large towns and issued their own currency, such as this gold coin made by the British Catuvellauni tribe in the first century BCE.

❹ HILLTOP FORTS

The Celts built fortified towns for protection. In some places, these were cliff-top enclosures made of stone. In others, they were hilltop forts, surrounded by huge banks of earth and protected by wooden walls. One of Europe's largest hilltop forts was at Maiden Castle in southwest Britain, shown here.

❺ WARRIORS AND WARFARE

Celtic tribes regularly launched raiding missions against each other to capture precious goods, food, and slaves. The chiefs maintained their elite status through warfare and the display of expensive craft objects, such as weapons and jewellery. Warriors were highly respected in Celtic society and were buried with their weapons and chariots. This bronze fitting from a war chariot was forged into the shape of a horse's head.

❻ WEAPONS

The Celts fought using heavy swords made from iron, and lighter spears, javelins, and daggers, such as the one shown here. They protected themselves with iron helmets and shields made of wood and leather. They also used intimidation to try to gain an edge over their opponents. They would blow loud war trumpets and paint their faces and bodies in blue paint, known as *wood*, before a battle.

❼ DEMISE AND SURVIVAL

Rome's expansion saw Celtic tribes conquered in Italy in 191 BCE, in Spain in 133 BCE, and in Gaul in 51 BCE. In the first century CE, the tribes of England were also taken over, despite fierce resistance by Celtic rulers, such as Boudicca. However, those Celts living in Scotland and Ireland managed to resist and so held on to their culture.

❽ VILLAGES AND ROUND HOUSES

The Celts spent most of their time farming and hunting. The houses in their villages were made of whatever was close to hand. In rocky or mountainous areas, they used stone, but in the lowlands of Europe, they used wood. In Britain, the Celts built round houses, such as this one, made of a timber frame with a thatched roof.

Boudicca led the Iceni against the Romans in the first century CE

TERRACOTTA ARMY
These life-size clay figures were built to guard the first Chinese emperor in the afterlife, following his death in 210 BCE. There are more than 8,000 figures in total, many in different poses.

Asia

EARLY INDIAN CIVILIZATIONS

The earliest civilization on the Indian subcontinent emerged on the flood plains of the Indus River Valley in the third millennium BCE. The people there created complicated irrigation systems and founded large cities. However, in the second millennium BCE, the Indus civilization disappeared taking many of its secrets with it. Later in the millennium, a new civilization developed in the Ganges River Valley. This saw great cultural advances, including the emergence of Buddhism, Hinduism, and Sanskrit.

▼ EARLY SETTLEMENT

Farming began in the Indus Valley in around 4000 BCE and was dependent on the annual flooding of the river. As crops increased, so the Indus people grew more sophisticated. They developed their own pottery, writing system, and trading networks. By 2600 BCE, the flood plain was home to more than 2,000 towns, the largest of which are shown below.

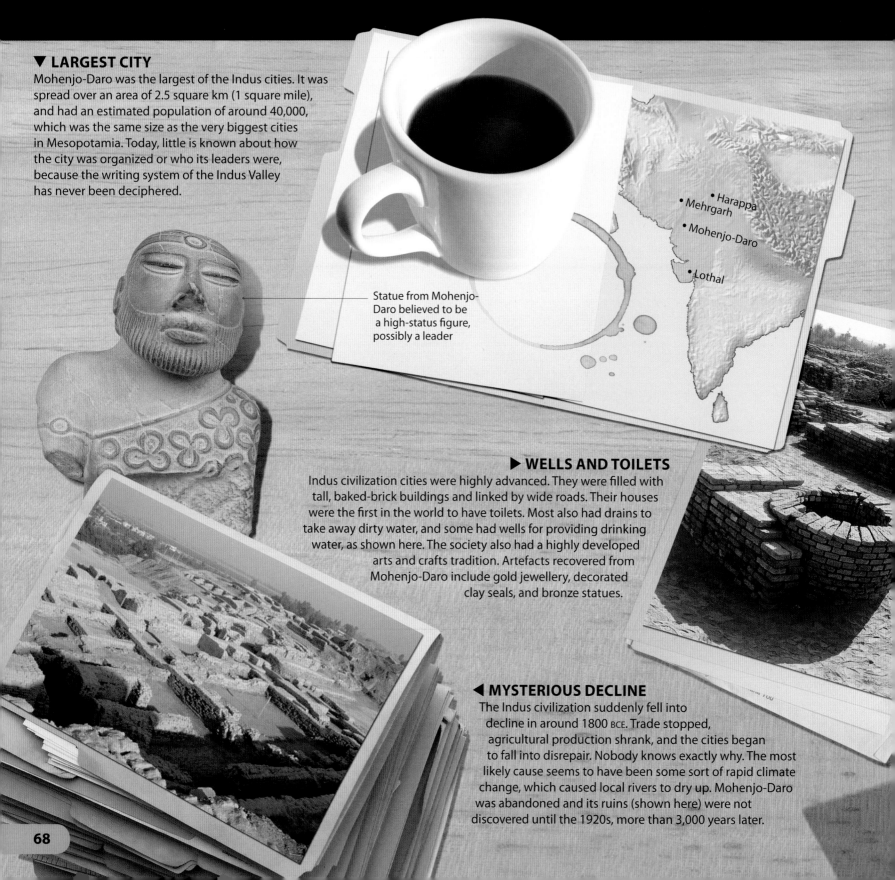

▼ LARGEST CITY

Mohenjo-Daro was the largest of the Indus cities. It was spread over an area of 2.5 square km (1 square mile), and had an estimated population of around 40,000, which was the same size as the very biggest cities in Mesopotamia. Today, little is known about how the city was organized or who its leaders were, because the writing system of the Indus Valley has never been deciphered.

Statue from Mohenjo-Daro believed to be a high-status figure, possibly a leader

- Harappa
- Mehrgarh
- Mohenjo-Daro
- Lothal

▶ WELLS AND TOILETS

Indus civilization cities were highly advanced. They were filled with tall, baked-brick buildings and linked by wide roads. Their houses were the first in the world to have toilets. Most also had drains to take away dirty water, and some had wells for providing drinking water, as shown here. The society also had a highly developed arts and crafts tradition. Artefacts recovered from Mohenjo-Daro include gold jewellery, decorated clay seals, and bronze statues.

◀ MYSTERIOUS DECLINE

The Indus civilization suddenly fell into decline in around 1800 BCE. Trade stopped, agricultural production shrank, and the cities began to fall into disrepair. Nobody knows exactly why. The most likely cause seems to have been some sort of rapid climate change, which caused local rivers to dry up. Mohenjo-Daro was abandoned and its ruins (shown here) were not discovered until the 1920s, more than 3,000 years later.

▼ GANGES CIVILIZATION

The region's next major culture started in the Ganges River Valley. It was founded by nomadic cattle herders from Central Asia, who migrated into India in around 1500 BCE. By 1000 BCE, they had settled down to farming and were living in villages. As their society became more complex, so the villages and towns merged to form 16 kingdoms known as *Mahajanapadas* (shown below). Gradually, one of these kingdoms, Magadha, became dominant.

▼ SANSKRIT

By 500 BCE, the Ganges civilization covered most of northern India. More is known about these people because their writing can be read. The Ganges people developed a written language, called Sanskrit, based on the Semitic script of the Middle East.

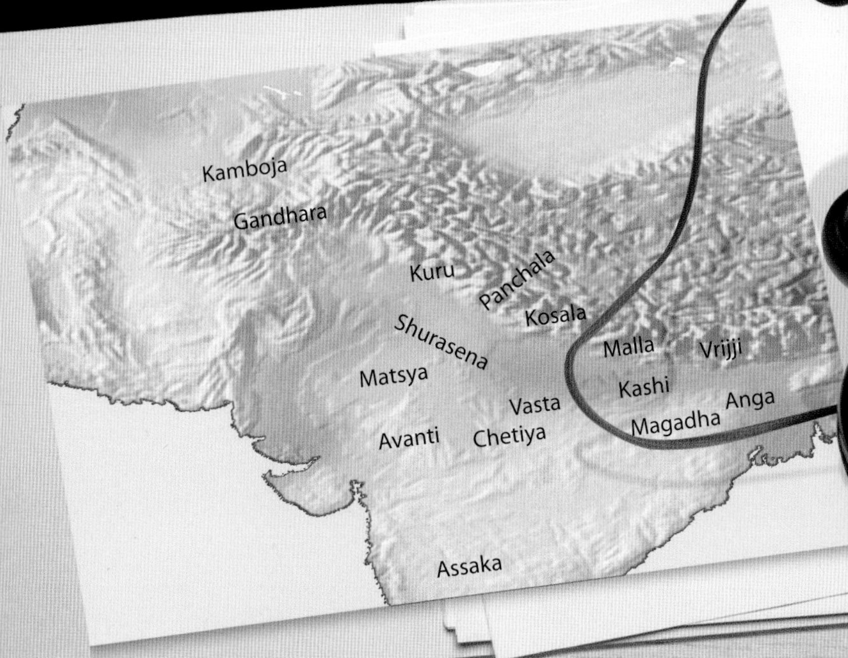

Kamboja

Gandhara

Kuru

Panchala

Shurasena

Kosala

Matsya

Malla

Vriji

Kashi

Vasta

Anga

Avanti

Chetiya

Magadha

Assaka

An example of Classical Sanskrit, which eventually replaced Vedic Sanskrit.

▼ BUDDHISM

This period saw the emergence of Buddhism, a religion based on the fifth century BCE teachings of Siddhartha Gautama, a Nepalese prince. The prince gave up his privileged lifestyle to try to find a way to escape suffering and sickness. Eventually, he achieved Enlightenment, a blissful state free of suffering. He spent the rest of his life teaching his beliefs. Buddha means "Enlightened one".

◀ THE VEDAS

The Ganges civilization devised an early form of Hinduism, which would become the predominant religion of India. Hindu beliefs were enshrined in four holy books known as the *Vedas*. These were composed using the writing system of the Ganges people, which came to be known as Vedic Sanskrit.

Agni is one of the most important Vedic gods

THE MAURYAN EMPIRE

The power of the mahajanapadas, the great kingdoms formed during the time of the Ganges civilization, had ended when the Mauryan Dynasty emerged in 321 BCE. The first Mauryan ruler, Chandragupta Maurya, conquered the Indus Valley, while his successors expanded Mauryan territory to take in most of India. The greatest Mauryan leader of all, Ashoka, converted to Buddhism and tried to encourage his subjects to do likewise, leading to a resurgence of the religion.

The Buddhist emperor Ashoka shown in a meditative pose

▶ ASHOKA

Chandragupta Maurya's son, Bindusara, expanded the empire into southern India. His successor, Ashoka, was even more acquisitive, taking control of a vast band of territory. It ranged from Afghanistan in the west to Bangladesh in the east, and stretched almost to the southern tip of India. He spent eight years on the warpath, culminating in the conquest of the kingdom of Kalinga in eastern India in 261 BCE.

According to legend, Chandragupta Maurya was the son of peacock tamers

Ashoka erected hundreds of pillars encouraging his subjects to live moral lives. Only 19 of these survive

▲ THE FIRST EMPEROR

Chandragupta Maurya came to power when he seized the throne of Magadha, then the most powerful mahajanapada. Perhaps fearful that someone might do something similar to him, he became a very paranoid man. He kept a bodyguard of 700 women (whom he trusted more than men), never slept in the same bed twice, and always employed a food taster. In 293 BCE, he retired to become a monk of the pacifist Jain religion.

◀ MORAL RULE

The death toll and bloodshed of Kalinga left Ashoka shocked, and prompted his conversion to Buddhism. In line with Buddhist teachings, the emperor decided to abandon his violent ways, and tried to rule by moral authority and reason, rather than by force. To this end, he had inscriptions urging non-violence and vegetarianism carved into rock faces and pillars across the empire. He also helped his subjects by renovating roads, improving irrigation channels, and building universities and hospitals.

▶ ASHOKA'S LEGACY

Despite his attempts to bring lasting change to India, Ashoka's achievements were quickly reversed. Most of his subjects would not convert to Buddhism, and Hinduism remained the dominant religion. After his death, his empire began to contract. The last Mauryan emperor was killed in 184 BCE and India once again fragmented. Ashoka's reputation, however, grew as the centuries passed. Today he is regarded as one of India's greatest leaders.

▼ BUDDHA'S GREAT PROMOTER

One of the most significant aspects of Ashoka's rule was his promotion of Buddhism. He was the first ruler to do so on a major scale, building thousands of Buddhist monasteries, *stupas* (buildings for housing the Buddha's sacred relics), and *viharas* (shelters for wandering monks) across his empire. He also sent missionaries abroad to other kingdoms and empires, including China, to spread Buddhist teachings. These helped to transform Buddhism into a major, international religion.

Pillar erected by Ashoka featuring the Ashoka chakra, a wheel representing the path to Enlightenment

Commissioned by Ashoka, the stupa at Sanchi in northern India is an important site of Buddhist pilgrimage

THE GUPTA EMPIRE

After the demise of the Mauryan empire, India reverted to a collection of regional kingdoms for about 400 years. In the third century CE, a new, powerful dynasty took control in Magadha under the rule of King Sri Gupta (240–280 CE). His successors formed a great empire, extending right across northern India. The empire eventually collapsed in the fifth century CE following an attack from the Huna people of Central Asia.

Ruins of a Gupta-era temple in Sanchi, northern India

▼ RISE OF THE GUPTA EMPIRE

The Gupta empire began with the accession to the throne of Chandragupta I in 320 CE. He increased his dynasty's power by conquest and through his marriage to the princess of a neighbouring kingdom. More territory was taken over by his son Samudragupta (335–375 CE). He defeated a number of the region's states, which were subsequently incorporated into the empire.

▼ CHANDRAGUPTA II

The high point of the empire came under the rule of Chandragupta II (380–413 CE). He extended the dynasty's territory from coast to coast. Like the Mauryan emperors before him, he ruled from Pataliputra. He also founded a second capital at Ujjain. Chandragupta was a great patron of arts, architecture, and literature, and his reign saw many works of art produced, such as those shown below.

▼ INTERNATIONAL TRADE

Trade increased greatly during the Gupta era. India became an important stop-off on the Silk Road from China to Europe. Indian merchants traded ivory, cashmere, cotton, and spices with their Chinese counterparts in return for silk. They also traded with the Roman empire, which helped to spread Indian culture. Trade also encouraged the use of money, such as this gold coin showing Chandragupta II on horseback.

▶ THE MONK'S VIEW

In the fourth century CE, a Chinese Buddhist monk called Faxian visited the empire of Chandragupta II. He described the Gupta capital, Pataliputra, as a great city, and Chandragupta as a just leader who looked after the poor: "The king governs without decapitation or [other] corporal punishments. Criminals are simply fined, lightly or heavily, according to the circumstances." Faxian would have dressed similarly to this modern monk.

▼ HINDU REVIVAL

Although Buddhism continued to be practised by a minority of the people, Hinduism was firmly established as the dominant religion in this period. Many of the *puranas* (sacred texts telling the history of the Universe and gods) were written at this time. Gupta society was divided into classes, or castes, according to Hindu teaching. Many temples were built, including the sixth-century Vishnu temple at Deorgarh, one of the earliest stone temples.

Stonework from the temple at Deorgarh

▲ KALIDASA

The most famous writer of the age was the poet-playwright Kalidasa. He is believed to have lived at some point in the fourth or fifth century CE and wrote numerous plays for the royal court. His most famous work is *Sakuntala*, a love story involving gods, a king, the daughter of a sage, and a curse of forgetfulness. This picture shows a scene from the play.

Galangal

Gingseng

▶ MEDICINE

The ancient Gupta Indians practised quite advanced medical techniques for the time. They knew how to make inoculations against smallpox and how to deliver babies by Caesarian section. They could use more than 500 medicinal plants, such as castor, ginseng, and galangal. Doctors performed basic forms of surgery, such as treating wounds and repairing broken bones.

Castor

Aryabhata the mathematician

▲ CLASSICAL AGE OF INDIA

The Gupta period saw a flourishing of scholarship and artistic achievements. Great advances were made in the fields of Sanskrit literature, the visual arts, science, mathematics, medicine, and astronomy. The period, which lasted until the invasion of the Huna in the fifth century CE, is sometimes called India's "golden age". Notable figures of the time include the Hindu mathematician Aryabhata.

EARLY CHINESE CIVILIZATIONS

The origins of the great Chinese civilization can be traced back to around 6500 BCE, when rice was first cultivated on the banks of the Yangtze river. Over the next few thousand years, the people grew increasingly sophisticated, creating elaborate irrigation systems that led to more complex forms of social organization. Eventually, China came under the control of two powerful dynasties: the Shang in the second millennium BCE, followed by the Zhou in the first millennium BCE. These dynastic periods saw great cultural advances, including the development of the Chinese script.

▼ EARLY DAYS
China's first significant culture was founded by the millet-farming Yangshao people of the Yellow River Basin in around 5000 BCE. Because millet has fewer nutrients than rice, the Yangshao did not develop an advanced society. By 3200 BCE, they were replaced by the more sophisticated, rice-growing Longshan Culture. The Longshan people produced intricate pieces of pottery, such as this bowl depicting a dragon.

▲ SHANG DYNASTY
From the second millennium BCE until the 20th century CE, China was dominated by a succession of powerful families, known as dynasties. The first major dynasty, the Shang, emerged in around 1800 BCE. Under the Shang, the Chinese became master bronze casters, making intricately crafted items, such as this ceremonial cup with handles in the shape of birds.

▲ SONS OF HEAVEN
This is a picture of King Tang who, according to Chinese legend, founded the Shang Dynasty in 1766 BCE. Shang kings were known as the "Sons of Heaven". They were regarded as both political and religious leaders, acting as intermediaries between the people and the gods. For several hundred years, the Shang Dynasty built up its power, taking control of a large area made up of numerous cities around the Yellow river.

▲ ORACLE BONES
Ancestor worship lay at the very heart of Shang society. The rulers consulted the royal ancestors before making decisions. They often did this by writing a question on an animal bone or a tortoise shell, and then striking it with a hot metal implement, cracking it. The cracks were then interpreted to give an answer.

▶ CHINESE WRITING

According to legend, Chinese writing was invented in the third millennium BCE by a government official called Cang Jie, who devised his system by copying animal tracks. However, the writing system probably developed later than this, under the Shang Dynasty. The earliest examples of writing, such as this inscription on a bronze vessel, date from around 1500 BCE, by which time there were more than 2,000 characters.

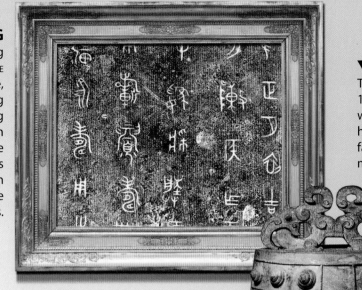

▼ ZHOU CHINA

The Shang Dynasty was overthrown in around 1000 BCE by King Wu of Zhou. He founded what would become the longest dynasty in Chinese history, lasting some 700 years. The Zhou royal family was based in the city of Xian, in the modern-day province of Shaanxi, and ruled over a network of fiefdoms controlled by royal dukes. Over time, these dukes became more powerful, while the kings grew weaker, eventually leading to a civil war known as the Warring States Period.

This bronze bell was made during the late Zhou period between 400–221 BCE

◀ CONFUCIANISM

During the Zhou Dynasty, two major belief systems emerged. The first of these was Confucianism, named after the teachings of the philosopher Confucius (551–479 BCE). He believed people should obey the law, do whatever the emperor and government told them to, and have respect for their families and ancestors. In return, the government should promise never to abuse its people.

▲ DAOISM

The other new belief system of the Zhou period was Daoism. This was inspired by the teachings of Lao Zi, a philosopher who lived in the sixth century BCE. He believed that people should live in harmony with nature. His beliefs, which are explained in his book, the *Daodejing*, are represented by the yin yang sign, which symbolizes balance.

THE FIRST EMPEROR

In the third century BCE, following a long period of civil war, China was united under the rule of King Zheng, who became its first emperor. He secured his power by abolishing the old states and deporting their rulers. His cruelty and ruthlessness, as well as the high taxes he raised to pay for his many building projects, made him very unpopular. When he died, the rest of the royal family were executed. However, the centralized system of government he established survived for more than 2,000 years.

Eighteenth-century portrait of Qin Shi Huangdi, China's first emperor

Map showing the different states during Warring States Period c. 260 BCE

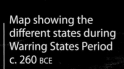

Yan
Zhao
Qi
Wei
Han
Chu
Qin

Little is known about Sun Tzu. It is thought that he lived during the Warring States Period between 480–226 BCE

▲ WARRING STATES PERIOD
At the end of the Zhou Dynasty's period of rule, China was divided into 17 states. These were ruled by dukes who were supposed to accept the authority of the Zhou kings. However, the weakness of the monarchy meant that many dukes now thought of themselves as independent rulers. In 480 BCE, the states went to war for the control of China. By 256 BCE, there were just seven states left. The strongest of these was Qin in western China.

▲ THE ART OF WAR
During the Warring States Period, a general named Sun Tzu wrote a guide to warfare known as *The Art of War*. One of Sun Tzu's main points was that a general had to learn as much as possible about the enemy before battle and work out a careful plan. However, the general also had to be able to change that plan quickly if the battle was not going well. Fooling the enemy was very important. Sun Tzu wrote, "All warfare is based on tricks and lies."

▲ THE FIRST EMPEROR
The leader of the state of Qin, King Zheng (246–210 BCE) defeated all the other states and united China under his control. Zheng took the new name of Qin Shi Huangdi, which means "First Emperor", and abolished the old states to make sure they would never be able to rise up against him. He then divided China up into new areas known as commanderies. To help unify the country, he made sure everyone used the same coins, weights, measurements, and writing scripts.

◄ IMPERIAL SERVICE

Qin Shi Huangdi further increased his power by abolishing the old aristocracy. In the new Chinese empire, leaders and government officials would get their jobs by passing exams, not by belonging to a certain family. Huangdi's successors created an enormous imperial civil service to run the country.

▼ TERRACOTTA ARMY

The emperor was obsessed with preparing for the afterlife and had an enormous tomb built for himself at his capital, Xian. In a pit next to the tomb stood more than 8,000 terracotta figures, including soldiers, horses, acrobats, and musicians, made to accompany and protect the emperor in the next life. All the figures were lifesize and the soldiers carried real metal weapons.

Chinese dragon carved from jade to form part of a scabbard

▲ GREAT WALL OF CHINA

The emperor used slave labour on a number of giant building projects, including canals, roads, and the enormous Epang Palace in Xian. The greatest of these projects saw thousands of slaves linking together a series of earth barriers to form a "Great Wall" aimed at keeping out invaders from the north. Many slaves died during its construction. It was rebuilt using stone and brick in the 15th century CE under the Ming Dynasty and stretches for 6,260 km (3,890 miles).

The wall is more than 5 m (17 ft) wide and more than 9 m (30 ft) high in places. Little of the original Qin wall survives

▲ CHINESE DRAGONS

Ever since the time of Qin Shi Huangdi, Chinese emperors have been associated with dragons. The first emperor chose the dragon as his symbol because the creature is regarded in China as the "lord of the water" and water was the Qin's lucky element. Dragons were believed to live in all lakes, rivers, and seas, as well as in rain clouds. Unlike in western cultures, Chinese dragons are not scary creatures but helpful ones, symbolizing wisdom, strength, and goodness.

THE CHINESE WAY

The ancient Chinese made significant advances in the fields of science, medicine, mathematics, and astronomy. They also developed a huge range of technological innovations, including paper, silk, and the compass. In later centuries, they invented gunpowder, fireworks, paper money, and porcelain. These not only improved their society, but also left a lasting legacy on the world.

◄ THE COMPASS

It is believed that the Chinese invented the compass in the third century BCE, not to find their way around, but to help them plan their towns. Early compasses were made of a naturally occurring magnetic rock called lodestone. In later centuries, the Chinese developed a navigational compass made from a magnetized needle floating in a bowl of water.

The first compasses had a central spoon that pointed south

▲ PAPER

According to legend, paper was invented in the early second century CE by Cai Lun, an official of the imperial court. It was made by mixing a fibrous material – originally silk, later wood – with water to form a pulp. A screen was dipped into the mixture, as shown above, collecting a thin layer of fibres. The water would then be squeezed out and the screen left to dry, forming a sheet of paper.

This silk banner dates from 186 BCE

The longer handles make it easier to lift the load

▲ WHEELBARROWS

Known as the "wooden ox" in China, the wheelbarrow was invented around 2,000 years ago. This simple device, consisting of a wheel, a basket, and a pair of handles, allowed people to transport heavy loads quickly and easily. The oldest picture of a wheelbarrow dates back to 118 CE.

◄ SILK

Made from threads taken from cocoons of the mulberry moth, silk was first woven in China in around 3000 BCE. Its export to other cultures led to the creation of a trans-continental trade network, the Silk Road. Chinese emperors tried to keep the knowledge of how silk was made a secret, but eventually other countries started producing their own silk.

◀ KITES

The development of silk made possible another invention: the kite. Silk was used for both the main sail and the flying lines, while bamboo poles provided lightweight support struts. The first kites were probably flown in the fifth century BCE and were used for a variety of different purposes, including testing wind speeds and military communications.

Like this modern version, the Chinese decorated their kites with colourful designs

Chinese crossbows were wooden with bronze triggers

▲ THE CROSSBOW

The crossbow could fire metal bolts with enormous force. They proved so effective that they put an end to chariot charges because riders could be killed before they reached the enemy's lines. The Chinese used giant crossbows, handheld crossbows, and repeating crossbows, which could fire large numbers of bolts in quick succession. The earliest Chinese crossbow dates back to the fifth century BCE.

▼ THE EARTHQUAKE FINDER

One of the most unusual Chinese inventions was the Earthquake Finder. China suffered numerous earthquakes every year, but it often took the Imperial capital several days to discover exactly where an earthquake had occurred. In 130 CE, Zhang Heng, the director of astrology under the Han Dynasty, devised a contraption that would show in which direction the earthquake had struck.

Chinese mould for casting sickle blades from the fifth century BCE

A ball would drop from a dragon's mouth to a frog's mouth to show the earthquake's direction

◀ CAST IRON

The Chinese began using iron in around 500 BCE, which was later than civilizations in India, the Middle East, and Europe. However, they developed a new, more technically advanced method for making tools – casting iron. Using bellows, Chinese metal-workers were able to get their furnaces much hotter than those in western civilizations. This allowed them to create liquid iron, which could then be poured into moulds to create weapons and tools.

ANCIENT KOREA

The first nomadic peoples arrived in Korea some time before 8000 BCE, eventually settling down to farming in the third millennium BCE. Korea's development was hugely influenced by its much bigger neighbour, China. Not only did China have an enormous impact on Korean art, architecture, and religion, but the two also fought each other regularly. In turn, the Korean kingdoms influenced other civilizations, particularly Japan.

▲ EARLY KOREA

Korean culture grew more sophisticated in the first millennium BCE. The people began burying their dead in large stone tombs known as *goindols*, and started using bronze weapons and tools from around the eighth century BCE onwards. Between the seventh and the fourth century BCE, a loose group of villages in the northwest of the peninsula joined together to form the first Korean kingdom, Gojoseon.

Koguryo

• Seoul

Silla

Paekche

▲ CHINESE COMMANDERIES

In 108 BCE, Gojoseon was invaded and taken over by China. The Chinese established four territories, known as commanderies, in Korea. Three were soon recaptured by the Koreans, but one, Lelang Commandery, lasted until the fourth century CE. Through Lelang, the Koreans were introduced to Chinese metalworking skills, bureaucratic systems, religious beliefs, and artworks, such as this lacquer box produced at Lelang.

◀ THE THREE KINGDOMS

Problems within China allowed a more independent Korea to emerge from the first century CE onwards. Although the Lelang Commandery remained under Chinese control for a couple of centuries more, elsewhere, the Korean chiefdoms gradually joined together to form three kingdoms. These were Silla in the southeast, Paekche in the southwest, and Koguryo in the north.

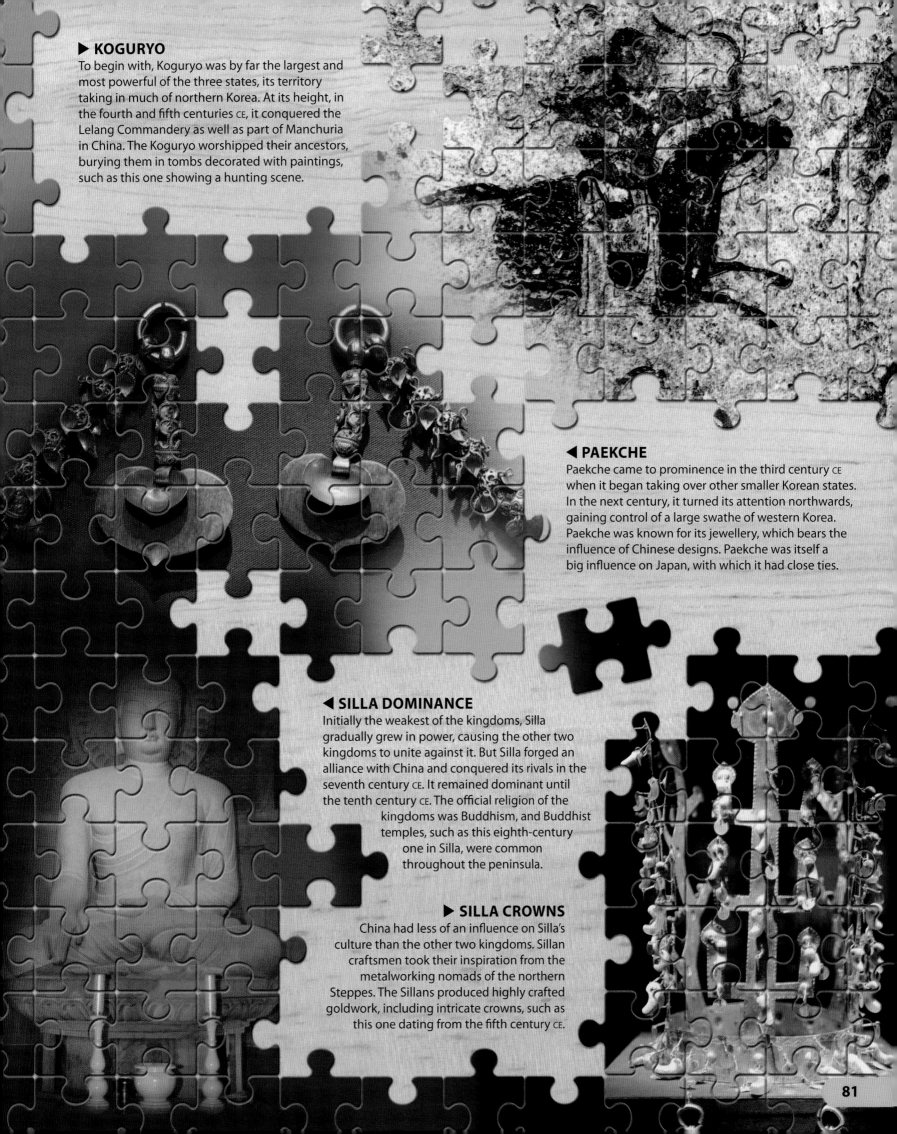

▶ KOGURYO

To begin with, Koguryo was by far the largest and most powerful of the three states, its territory taking in much of northern Korea. At its height, in the fourth and fifth centuries CE, it conquered the Lelang Commandery as well as part of Manchuria in China. The Koguryo worshipped their ancestors, burying them in tombs decorated with paintings, such as this one showing a hunting scene.

◀ PAEKCHE

Paekche came to prominence in the third century CE when it began taking over other smaller Korean states. In the next century, it turned its attention northwards, gaining control of a large swathe of western Korea. Paekche was known for its jewellery, which bears the influence of Chinese designs. Paekche was itself a big influence on Japan, with which it had close ties.

◀ SILLA DOMINANCE

Initially the weakest of the kingdoms, Silla gradually grew in power, causing the other two kingdoms to unite against it. But Silla forged an alliance with China and conquered its rivals in the seventh century CE. It remained dominant until the tenth century CE. The official religion of the kingdoms was Buddhism, and Buddhist temples, such as this eighth-century one in Silla, were common throughout the peninsula.

▶ SILLA CROWNS

China had less of an influence on Silla's culture than the other two kingdoms. Sillan craftsmen took their inspiration from the metalworking nomads of the northern Steppes. The Sillans produced highly crafted goldwork, including intricate crowns, such as this one dating from the fifth century CE.

ANCIENT JAPAN

The civilization of ancient Japan was a mixture of native culture and outside influences. For many thousands of years after the end of the last ice age, people on the Japanese islands lived an isolated existence, developing their own distinct lifestyles and customs. However, from around 300 BCE onwards, Japan came into close contact with the other major Asian civilizations, particularly China and Korea. This brought Japan new technologies and ideas, including rice-farming, iron-making, and Buddhism, to add to its own distinct traditions.

Jomon pots were simple handmade pieces that were set in fire rather than kilns

Yayoi pots were made using a potter's wheel

◀ FIRST PEOPLES
The first Japanese people, known as the Jomon, may have arrived as far back as 16,000 BCE. Although these early settlers were hunter-gatherers, Japan's rich food environment allowed them to live a semi-settled lifestyle. This enabled them to develop pottery, usually associated with farming cultures. In fact, the Jomon created what is believed to be the world's earliest pottery, dating back to the 14th millennium BCE.

◀ YAYOI
Migration from Korea and China in the late first millennium BCE helped to start the development of Japan's next significant culture, the Yayoi Culture. This emerged between 300 BCE–300 CE. This period saw the introduction of intensive rice cultivation in paddy fields, bronze weapons and tools, and more advanced pottery. The Yayoi people also built permanent villages where hierarchies emerged based on the control of food stores. These villages were ruled by chiefs.

The Izumo Taisha shrine was founded around 1,500 years ago, although the current building dates only from the 18th century

▼ SHINTO

From the Jomon Period onwards, the Japanese practised a religion known as Shinto. This involved the worship of both their ancestors and spirits, known as *kami*, that they believed resided in all things. Worship took place at shrines, which could be manmade, such as this one, or natural places, such as mountains, waterfalls, or groves of trees, where powerful kami could be found. Shinto is still widely followed in Japan today.

▼ BUDDHISM

Buddhism was introduced to Japan from China in the sixth century CE. It wasn't particularly popular to begin with, but started to attract more followers from the seventh century onwards as temples appeared throughout the country, such as the temple of Shitenno-ji at Osaka (shown here). However, Buddhism did not replace Shinto and both religions were practised side by side, as they are today.

The Yamato were buried with special objects known as *haniwa* for use in the afterlife, such as this horse

Bronze image of Buddha from the early seventh century CE, shortly after Buddhism had been introduced from China

◀ CHINESE INFLUENCE

The Yamato rulers and their successors were hugely influenced by the much older civilization of China. They based their imperial court and social organization on Chinese models, introduced a Chinese-style civil service based on merit, and adopted Chinese written symbols known as *kanji*. They also sent a number of diplomatic missions to China to bring back the latest Chinese goods and ideas. The last of these took place in 838 CE, after which a more distinctly Japanese culture emerged.

▲ YAMATO

In the early first millennium BCE, the Japanese people were divided into a number of clans. By the fourth century BCE, one of these clans, the Yamato, had become dominant over the rest of the country. Its chief became the country's first emperor. Members of the Yamato ruling class were buried in stone tombs beneath large earth mounds known as *kofuns*. The largest kofuns were more than 400 m (1,300 ft) long.

STEPPE NOMADS

In the first millennium BCE, trade increased between eastern civilizations, such as China, and the western civilizations of the Middle East and Europe. Much of this commerce was carried along routes that ran through the grassy plains of Central Asia, known as the Steppes. For hundreds of years, these trade routes were controlled by the nomadic Scythian people. Eventually, however, they were forced from their homeland by another nomadic people from the east, the Huns.

A seventh-century-BCE Scythian gold belt buckle showing fighting animals

Detail of a horse and rider from what is thought to be the oldest existing carpet in the world, dating back to the 5th century BCE

▲ SCYTHIAN GOLDWORK

The Scythians were famous for the quality of their crafts, particularly their goldwork, which they traded with many other cultures, including the Greeks. The demands of the Scythians' largely nomadic lifestyle meant that most of their art took the form of small, portable pieces. These were used for decorating horses, tents, weapons, and shields. Their designs usually featured the animals of the Steppes, including wolves, horses, bears, and big cats.

▲ KURGANS

The Scythians had no written language, so most of what we know about them comes from archaeology, and particularly their great burial mound sites known as *kurgans*. These warrior graves could be up to 20 m (65 ft) high and were filled with high-status goods, including goldwork. Items recovered from kurgans include Greek pottery, Chinese silk, and Middle Eastern carpets, showing just how extensive the Scythians' trading network was.

▲ SCYTHIANS

The Scythians were horse-riding nomads who are believed to have emerged in Iran in around 1000 BCE. Over the next few centuries, they expanded northwards and went on to dominate a vast area of the Central Asian Steppes, stretching from the Black Sea to Kazakhstan. They were renowned as fierce warriors. The fifth century BCE Greek historian Herodotus claimed that they liked to make cups out of the skulls of their enemies.

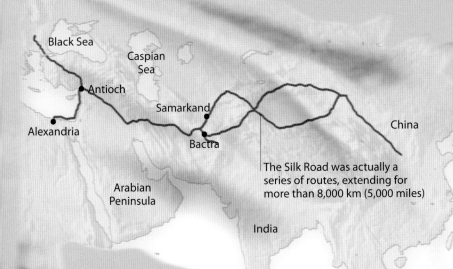

The Silk Road was actually a series of routes, extending for more than 8,000 km (5,000 miles)

The Visigoths celebrate after defeating the Huns in Gaul

▲ THE SILK ROAD

The Silk Road was the great trading link between China, India, Central Asia, the Middle East, and Europe. Goods, ideas, technologies, and cultural developments passed between the civilizations along this route. During their period of dominance, the Scythians played an important role on the Silk Road, helping merchants to travel through the areas they controlled, in return for a fee.

The Huns were highly skilled horsemen and fierce warriors. Here they are shown defeating a rival people, the Alans

▲ ADVANCE OF THE HUNS

In the fifth century CE, under the command of Attila, the Huns formed a mighty empire, reaching from the Steppes to Central Europe. But they had ambitions to take over even more territory and headed west. The Romans joined forces with a Germanic tribe, the Visigoths, to stop their advance in Gaul. However, Attila was aiming to conquer the Roman empire and pushed on into Italy.

According to legend, Attila was buried in a triple coffin made of gold, silver, and iron

▲ THE HUNS

The Scythians were eventually pushed west out of their heartland by the appearance of another nomadic people, the Huns. The Huns probably originated in western China. In the early first century CE, they started to migrate west, pushing the Scythians before them. This had a knock-on effect right across Asia and into Europe. In the fourth century CE, several Germanic tribes were pushed west out of their territory, forcing them into conflict with the Roman empire.

▲ COLLAPSE OF HUN EMPIRE

Attila's career of conquest was stopped when he died suddenly in 453 CE. His reign marked the brief high point of the Hun empire. After his death, the empire was supposed to be split between his three sons, but one, Ellac, seized control of it all. Ellac was defeated by another people, the Gepids, in 454 CE, after which the entire Hun empire crumbled away.

The Americas

THE OLMECS

In the first millennium BCE, the civilizations of Europe, North Africa, Asia, and the Middle East were in contact with each other through trade and warfare. However, on the American continents new civilizations were being created, which the rest of the world would know nothing about until the 15th century. The first of these were the Olmecs of Mesoamerica. Their development was started by the cultivation of maize, the Americas' main crop.

▼ CEREMONIAL CENTRES

The Olmecs founded their first towns in around 1500 BCE and soon after began constructing ceremonial centres with temples throughout their Central American heartland. The largest of these was San Lorenzo. These religious sites were also where the Olmecs kept stores of surplus food. It is not known for sure how early Olmec society was organized. However, it is believed that they lived in groups led by chiefs, who were also the religious leaders.

▶ ORIGINS & FARMING

The Olmecs began farming in the area that is today southern Mexico (see map), in around 2000 BCE. They grew crops on the banks of rivers that received nutrients through regular flooding, much as early civilizations in Egypt, India, and China. They also created fields by burning down sections of rainforest. The Olmecs' main crop was maize, but they also grew beans, squash, and sweet potatoes, and fished and hunted the local wildlife.

Maize kernels

Tres Zapotes

Laguna de los Cerros

La Venta

San Lorenzo

Etlatongo

San Jose Mogote

Olmec heartland

Olmec heartland

Southern Mexico

Stone sculpture from San Lorenzo dating to some time between 1200–900 BCE

Olmec carving of a were-jaguar, a religious creature that was half-man, half-jaguar

◀ ART STYLES

Much of what we know about the Olmecs comes from their highly stylized pieces of art. These were created from a variety of different materials, including stone, clay, and jade. Much of this art was clearly religious, often depicting strange, mythical creatures, such as the were-jaguar. They also made items in the shape of fish, serpents, and monkeys. All these creatures are believed to have played important roles in their religion.

▶ BIG HEADS

The most striking Olmec sculptures are the giant stone heads. Each head has unique features and is believed to represent a specific ruler. The biggest are more than 3 m (10 ft) tall and weigh 55 tonnes. They were made of a type of volcanic rock, which was brought from far away without the use of wheels, metal tools, or working animals, none of which were known to the early American civilizations.

◀ OLMEC INFLUENCE

Sometimes called the "mother culture of Mesoamerica", the Olmecs invented many of the practices followed by the region's later civilizations. These include ritual blood letting, the making of jade masks (shown here), the playing of a ceremonial ball game, and the use of a 260-day calendar. The Olmecs also invented what is thought to be the first writing system in the western hemisphere. The earliest example of this picture writing dates back to 1000–800 BCE.

Carved stone relief from La Venta

▶ TRADE

The Olmecs were by far the most advanced people in Mesoamerica in the first millennium BCE, but they did have contact with other peoples in the region, with whom they traded. They exchanged a variety of goods, including pottery, stone, shells, and tar, which was used to seal roofs and boats. This trade took place both on land and along rivers, and was probably one of the main ways in which the Olmec culture was spread around the continent.

Olmec pottery figure that would have been traded with other civilizations

◀ OLMEC DEMISE

Every few hundred years, the Olmecs destroyed their main ceremonial centre and created another in a different location. San Lorenzo was abandoned in around 900 BCE in favour of La Venta. This new centre thrived until 400 BCE when it too was replaced by Tres Zapotes. After this, however, the Olmec civilization slowly faded away, perhaps because the local rivers silted up or the rainforest soils were exhausted – no one knows for certain.

THE MAYA

The Maya were probably the most sophisticated of the civilizations in the Americas before the arrival of Europeans. They originated around 1200 BCE, taking control of much of Mesoamerica after the demise of the Olmecs. The civilization reached its peak from 300–800 CE, when the Maya created elaborate stone cities, and developed a complex society, as well as their own religion, writing system, and games. However, the civilization began to decline after this period.

▶ CEREMONIAL CENTRES

The Maya erected hundreds of ceremonial cities in the rainforests of Mesoamerica. These were usually built to the same pattern, with a palace for the ruler, a plaza for the marketplace, and several giant stone step pyramids. The cities shared the same culture, but remained separate from each other. There was never a single Mayan empire, but rather a widespread, interconnected civilization.

Priests performed religious ceremonies at the top of Mayan pyramids

◀ BALL GAME

Every Mayan city had a ball court. Here, a game was played with a hard rubber ball that seems to have been both a form of entertainment and an event of great religious significance. No one today knows exactly what the rules were, but it is thought that two teams competed to get the ball through a stone ring, without using their hands. Losers may have been put to death.

▶ FESTIVALS

The Maya celebrated a religious festival on every twentieth day. The priests, dressed in elaborate headdresses, would climb one of the city's step pyramids and give thanks to the gods. Accompanied by music and dancing, the priests would then sacrifice animals. They also performed blood-letting rituals when they would prick themselves with sharp implements, such as cactus spikes, offering their blood to the gods. Some rituals involved human sacrifice.

◀ MAYAN WRITING

The Maya created a writing system using around 700 symbols, or glyphs, each representing a sound, a word, or part of a word. Glyphs were used to record events on stone slabs called stelae. The Maya also created books, known as codices, made of soft bark pages that were folded like a fan. These told stories about Mayan gods and myths.

◀ MAYAN BELIEFS

The Maya saw the heavens, the Earth, and the underworld as one interconnected whole, at the centre of which was the "World Tree". The Maya worshipped many gods, who they believed controlled the natural forces. The jaguar was also important in Mayan beliefs. Priests often dressed as jaguars because they believed that jaguars had the power to cross from the normal world to the world of the gods.

▶ ASTRONOMY

The Maya believed that the world worked according to predictable rules that could be discovered through astronomy. They dedicated themselves to the study of the sky, particularly the Sun, the Moon, and Venus. This enabled them to develop a precise calendar, which they used to measure their years and to predict future astronomical events.

Temples were built to line up with certain events, such as sunrise, on particular days

▶ THE END

After 800 CE, many of the Mayan states began to collapse, possibly because of over-clearing of the forests, which led to desertification and massive crop failure. However, some Maya communities in Mexico continued to thrive until Spanish invaders arrived in the 16th century and took over the region. Many of the "lost" cities, such as Tikal (shown here), were swallowed up by the rainforest and were not rediscovered until modern times.

Teotihuacán's central road is known as the "Avenue of the Dead"

TEOTIHUACÁN AND THE TOLTECS

While the Maya were the dominant force in eastern Mexico, much of central Mexico came under the influence of the city of Teotihuacán (200 BCE–700 CE). After Teotihuacán's mysterious destruction, power in this region passed to a people called the Toltecs, who at their height controlled a great swathe of central and western Mexico. The Toltecs' distinctive culture proved a huge influence on the region's next and greatest power, the Aztecs.

❶ TEOTIHUACÁN

Teotihuacán was founded in around 200 BCE and grew to become one of the largest cities in the ancient world. During its greatest period, in around 450 CE, the city may have had a population of around 150,000–200,000, and it covered a larger area than ancient Rome. The city declined sharply from the sixth century CE onwards and was eventually abandoned.

❷ PYRAMIDS OF THE SUN AND MOON

At the centre of Teotihuacán are two huge pyramids. The largest of these is 71 m (233 ft) tall and consists of around 3 million tonnes of stone and brick, making it the largest structure in the Americas prior to the arrival of Europeans. The pyramids were later discovered by the Aztecs, who named them after the Sun and the Moon.

❸ SACRIFICE

Excavations below the Pyramid of the Moon have shown that sacrifices took place regularly during the building process. The people of Teotihuacán sacrificed both humans and powerful animals, such as pumas, wolves, eagles, falcons, and rattlesnakes. These sacrifices were probably made as a way of honouring the gods and getting them to bless each stage of the construction.

❹ TOLTECS

Following Teotihuacán's demise, a new people, the Toltecs, migrated into Mexico in around 900 CE. The Toltecs were a warlike tribe who quickly expanded throughout much of Mesoamerica, conquering many Mayan cities. This may have led to a partial fusion of the two cultures. There are a great many architectural similarities between the Toltec city of Tula and the Mayan city of Chichén Itzá, shown here.

❺ QUETZALCÓATL

Under the Toltecs' influence, the cult of the winged serpent god Quetzalcóatl spread throughout Mesoamerica. Later, the Aztecs told a legend about a Toltec leader, Topiltzin, who was believed to be the human incarnation of Quetzalcoatl. Topiltzin was banished from his kingdom and headed east to found a new kingdom. The Maya also told a similar legend about a leader named Kukulcán (Maya for Quetzalcoatl).

❻ TULA

By the 10th century CE, the Toltec capital of Tula had grown into one of Mexico's largest cities, home to more than 30,000 people. At the city's centre were various ceremonial structures, including step pyramids and ball courts. After the Toltec empire fell, the site was plundered by the Aztecs and many of its treasures were removed. A number of columns carved in the shape of Toltec warriors remain, however.

❼ ART

Toltec art often portrayed jungle creatures, such as snakes and jaguars, which played important roles in their lives and religion. One of the Toltecs' most distinctive artworks was the *chacmool*, a reclining figure holding a bowl or tray over its stomach. It is believed that the chacmool may have represented the Toltec rain god. The Toltec style of art greatly inspired the Aztecs.

Many Aztec artefacts, such as this mask, were based on styles devised by the Toltecs

❽ FALL OF TOLTEC EMPIRE

Tula was sacked and the Toltec empire fell in 1168. Their cultural legacy would be kept alive, however, by the region's next major arrivals, the Aztecs. The Aztecs hugely admired the Toltecs and saw themselves as successors to the Toltecs' great civilization. In fact, the word "Toltec" means "civilized" in Aztec. The Aztecs spoke the same regional language as the Toltecs, Nahuatl, and this allowed them to easily adopt the Toltec culture as their own.

THE AZTECS

The Aztecs were a nomadic people who arrived in the Valley of Mexico in around 1200 BCE. There were several other tribes already living there, and this forced the Aztecs to settle on a small island in Lake Texcoco. The Aztecs built a city, Tenochtitlán, on an island in the lake and this became the centre of their powerful empire. For over a hundred years, the Aztecs ruled much of Mesoamerica, until the arrival of the Spanish in 1519.

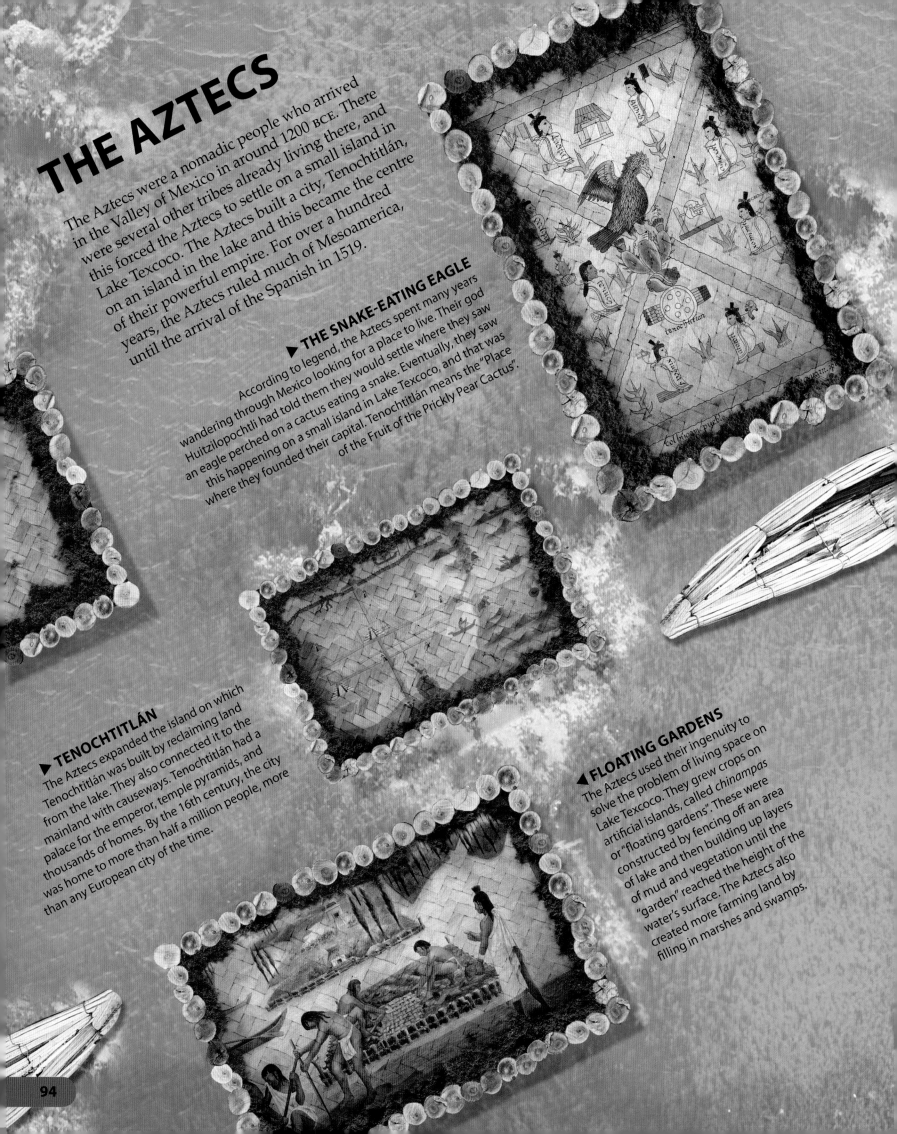

▶ THE SNAKE-EATING EAGLE

According to legend, the Aztecs spent many years wandering through Mexico looking for a place to live. Their god Huitzilopochtli had told them they would settle where they saw an eagle perched on a cactus eating a snake. Eventually, they saw this happening on a small island in Lake Texcoco, and that was where they founded their capital. Tenochtitlán means the "Place of the Fruit of the Prickly Pear Cactus".

▶ TENOCHTITLÁN

The Aztecs expanded the island on which Tenochtitlán was built by reclaiming land from the lake. They also connected it to the mainland with causeways. Tenochtitlán had a palace for the emperor, temple pyramids, and thousands of homes. By the 16th century, the city was home to more than half a million people, more than any European city of the time.

◀ FLOATING GARDENS

The Aztecs used their ingenuity to solve the problem of living space on Lake Texcoco. They grew crops on artificial islands, called chinampas or "floating gardens." These were constructed by fencing off an area of lake and then building up layers of mud and vegetation until the "garden" reached the height of the water's surface. The Aztecs also created more farming land by filling in marshes and swamps.

▼ EXPANSION

The Aztecs started to expand their territory from 1400 onwards. They took over the other tribes' land and demanded tribute from them in the form of food, clothes, precious objects, and people, who were sacrificed to appease the Aztec gods. To control their empire, the Aztecs built new cities that were ruled by nobles who were subject only to the Aztec emperor.

Extent of Aztec empire

Tenochtitlán

▼ MOCTEZUMA II

Moctezuma II, who came to the throne in 1502, was the greatest of the Aztec emperors. He was also one of the last. Under his rule, the Aztecs greatly increased their territory, conquering numerous tribes and demanding large amounts of tribute. This created a great deal of resentment among the conquered tribes. The Aztec empire reached its maximum size during his reign.

▼ FALL OF THE AZTECS

In 1519, Spanish invaders arrived in Mexico. Moctezuma II tried to make peace, inviting the new arrivals into Tenochtitlán. The Aztec people, however, revolted. Moctezuma II was killed, the city was sacked, and the Aztec empire was taken over by the Spanish. Millions of Aztecs died of diseases, such as smallpox, brought over by the Spanish, to which they had no immunity.

This picture shows the first meeting between Moctezuma II and the Spanish conqueror, Hernán Cortés

THE AZTEC WORLD

Warfare was important to Aztec society. Their empire was built and maintained by force, and every single Aztec male was given military training. The emperor was the supreme commander of the armed forces. Below him, the nobles provided most of the army's professional soldiers, while the commoners, who made up the majority of the population, offered military assistance when not farming the fields. Commoners could only rise in society through success in warfare, and specifically by taking captives for use as sacrifices.

▼ AZTEC RELIGION

The Aztecs had many gods but worshipped Huitzilopochtli, the god of the Sun and war, above all others. They believed that the gods could be satisfied through the sacrifice of animals, objects, and, in particular, people. Many of the victims of human sacrifice were prisoners of war. They were killed on top of massive temple pyramids.

Slaves were often put in wooden collars to make it difficult to escape

During a human sacrifice, the victim's still-beating heart was cut out with a flint knife

◀ AZTEC SLAVES

Aztec society relied on slave labour. Some slaves were prisoners of war, but many were Aztecs. People were not born slaves. Instead, they were made slaves because they had been found guilty of a crime or because they could not pay a debt. Sometimes, a poor freeperson might sell themself as a slave. This meant they no longer had to pay taxes or serve in the army. Slaves could also buy back their freedom.

▶ AZTEC LAW

As more people were incorporated into the Aztec empire, so there was a need for more laws. The punishments for breaking these laws could be very severe. Murderers, thieves, and anyone found drunk could be put to death. If criminals confessed their crime to a priest, they would be forgiven. However, they had to do this before they were caught and they could only do this once.

This stone statue of an Aztec priest dates from the 15th century

SCHOOLING ▼

To run their empire, the Aztecs needed a population that could do many jobs, so they provided free schooling for boys and girls. They were the only people in the world to do this at the time. The boys learned how to be soldiers, astronomers, engineers, doctors, and farmers, while the girls learned how to weave, cook, sew, and bring up children.

A teacher instructs pupils at a *calmecac*, a school for noble children

The emperor showed his status by wearing a headdress made from feathers

◄ SOCIAL STATUS

In Aztec times, the sort of house you lived in depended on your social status. The emperor had the grandest house, living in a vast palace in Tenochtitlán with its own zoo. Nobles also had large homes made of mud bricks or stone, while the poor lived in simple huts with thatched roofs. By law, only the nobles could live in houses more than one storey high.

ECONOMY ▼

Most towns had a market once a week, while at Tenochtitlán there was one every day. The commoners came here to trade food, clothes, and building materials. There were no coins in Aztec times. Instead cocoa beans were used for small purchases (an egg cost three beans) and lengths of cotton cloth known as *quachtli* were used for larger purchases.

The Aztecs made masks out of jade

▲ AZTEC ART

Aztec art was made mainly for religious reasons, as a way of honouring the gods. They decorated the walls of their temples with carvings and created enormous stone sculptures of their gods. They also fashioned much smaller pieces from jade and quartz. One of the Aztecs' most famous sculptures is the calendar stone, a disc showing the Sun god.

▶ AZTEC WRITING

The picture to the right shows an example of the Aztecs' simple writing system. It was made up of pictograms, which the Aztecs used to create calendars, accounts, and basic records of events. The writing has survived in books written on bark known as codices. These were written by the Aztecs, but supervised by the Spanish after the conquest. Those written before the Spanish arrival were destroyed.

97

EARLY SOUTH AMERICAN CULTURES

Most ancient civilizations emerged after the development of farming. The first complex societies in South America, however, were based instead on fishing. In the third millennium BCE, seafood was so plentiful off the coast of Peru that surpluses were created, allowing labour to be used for creating ceremonial centres and temples. Farming didn't become widespread in the Andes until the second millennium BCE with the development of terracing – cutting flat levels into steep slopes in order to grow crops in mountain terrain.

▶ CONFLICT

The second millennium BCE saw the development of farming, pottery, and art. It also saw increased interaction and trade between the fishing communities of the coast and the farming communities of the interior. This seems to have brought the communities into conflict, as shown by discoveries at the inland urban centre of Cerro Sechin where engraved stone slabs show warriors going to battle (shown here) and the execution of prisoners.

▲ AMERICA'S FIRST CITY

The first civilization in the Americas emerged in northern Peru in around 2600 BCE. Here, the fishing community of Aspero was founded on the coast, while just inland the settlement of Caral grew to become what has been called the "first city of the New World". The people of Caral built a number of large earth pyramids (shown here), although they did not develop pottery.

▶ CHAVÍN

From 800 BCE onwards a new people, the Chavín, began to dominate much of the central Andes. Their culture emerged out of the urban centre of Chavín de Huantar, which was filled with sophisticated stone architecture. Its main temple pyramid contained a dagger-shaped rock known as the Lanzon. This is believed to represent the Chavín's supreme deity. The site was a major centre of pilgrimage for the region's peoples.

► CHAVÍN ART

The Chavín developed a highly influential style of art. They decorated their temples with large carvings of jaguars, eagles, and other rainforest animals. They also worked on smaller objects, creating highly crafted items, such as the ornate pot shown here, conch-shell trumpets, spoons, and bottles, which they would bury with their dead. The Chavín were one of first people in the region to use metals in their art. Their culture declined around 200 BCE.

▼ MUMMIES

The Chinchorro people of the Chilean Andes were the first people in the world to preserve their dead as mummies, starting in around 5000 BCE, well before the practice began in ancient Egypt. The preservation process involved replacing the corpse's skin with clay and the internal organs with animal hair. The mummy was then buried in the dry ground of the Andes. The practice was later adopted by many of the region's other cultures.

▲ THE PARACAS

The Paracas was an Andean fishing culture that arose on the Peruvian coast between 600 BCE and 175 CE. Today, these people are renowned for the high quality of their textiles. Most of what we know about the Paracas comes from a large necropolis filled with mummies that was discovered in 1920. Each mummy was wrapped in finely woven cloth that was decorated with bright patterns.

MOCHE AND NAZCA

The Chavín culture was replaced in around 100 CE by the Moche, who founded South America's first great state on Peru's northern coast. They created large ceremonial centres filled with tall mud brick pyramids. Further south, the Nazca marked out enormous drawings of animals and shapes on the ground. The states that emerged after the Moche's decline, Wari and Tiwanaku, took over even more territory, building large rival empires that covered stretches of coast, lowland, and mountain.

▼ MOCHE ART

The Moche were skilled weavers, metalworkers, and, in particular, potters. They created a huge range of very detailed ceramic vessels often in the shape of animals, such as deer and condors, which may have represented characters from their myths. Many pots have been recovered from gravesites – the higher the status of individual, the more elaborate the pottery. The Moche also indulged in body art, such as tattoos.

▼ THE MOCHE

The Moche were highly skilled farmers, building a network of irrigation channels in the region's river valleys to feed their fields of maize. It's not known whether the Moche were an empire under a single government or a collection of separate, but interconnected, urban units, like the Maya. However, what is certain is that their society collapsed between 600–800 CE, caused, it is believed, by local climate change.

The Moche buried their leaders in tombs surrounded by jewellery and weapons made of gold, silver, and copper

◄ SUN AND MOON PYRAMIDS

At the centre of the Moche state lay two great adobe step pyramids dedicated to the Sun and the Moon. The largest, the Pyramid of the Sun (shown here), stood more than 50 m (160 ft) tall. Each of the thousands of mud bricks used to build the pyramid bears the stamp of the local community that provided it. The pyramids were the setting for the Moche's bloodthirsty religious practices, which involved human sacrifice and possibly even cannibalism.

Many Moche pots had spouts, such as this vessel in the shape of a frog

◄ THE NAZCA

The Nazca evolved out of the earlier Paracas culture along the southern coast of Peru in around 100 CE. They developed highly advanced craft skills, particularly textile making and pottery, which often featured depictions of sea creatures. Like the Moche, the Nazca culture declined in around 800 CE, again probably because of local climate change.

► TIWANAKU

New regional powers emerged as Moche and Nazca power faded. One of the most significant was centred on the great city of Tiwanaku. The people here were skilled farmers. Between 600–800 CE, they took over much of the Chilean Andes, but the society collapsed in around 1000 CE, probably due to a long drought.

▲ NAZCA LINES

The Nazca drew giant pictures of animals and birds on the ground known as geoglyphs or Nazca lines. The biggest measure more than 200 m (650 ft). They were made by removing dark coloured pebbles at the surface to reveal the white ground below. No one knows exactly why the Nazca created these enormous images, but they were probably designed to be seen from above by the gods.

Nazca line pictures representing a spider and a hummingbird

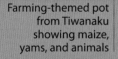

Farming-themed pot from Tiwanaku showing maize, yams, and animals

► WARI

Tiwanaku's great northern rival was the city of Wari, which controlled the Peruvian Andes, including the former lands of the Moche and Nazca people. The Wari made great advances in terrace agriculture and road-building. These were later adopted by the Incas. The drought that destroyed Tiwanaku also caused the Wari civilization to collapse in around 1000 CE.

Ceremonial Wari hat made of feathers, decorated with images of jungle cats

THE INCAS

Between the third and the 15th century CE, the states of the South American Andes grew larger and more powerful. The largest and most powerful of all was the Inca empire. It expanded rapidly during the 15th century, bringing most of the Andean region, and some 12 million people, under its control. The Incas were the first people in the region to start using metal weapons and tools.

❶ CHIMÚ

After the rival empires of Tiwanaku and Wari collapsed in the 11th century CE, a number of smaller states emerged. The next major power wouldn't arrive until the 13th century when the Chimú civilization emerged on Peru's northern coast. At its mud brick capital of Chan Chan (shown below), an elite of nobles ruled over an estimated population of 70,000. The Chimú empire was conquered by the Incas in 1470.

❷ RISE OF THE INCAS

For the first two centuries of their existence, from 1200 onwards, the Incas remained a small tribe based at the minor town of Cuzco. That changed, however, after the ruler Pachacutec (1438–1471) claimed to have received a vision of the creator god Viracocha telling him to do "great deeds". In just a couple of decades, Pachacutec and his son Tupac Yupanqui expanded their empire until it covered most of the Andean region.

❸ MANCO CÁPAC

Inca legends name the very first Inca as Manco Cápac. He was the son of the Sun god and was sent to Earth with a gold staff and instructions to build a temple at the place where he could sink the staff into the ground. The temple, the Coricancha, was regarded by the Incas as the centre of the Universe and lay at the heart of Cuzco.

Cuzco

❹ CUZCO

The Incas called their empire Tawantinsuyu, or "Land of the Four Quarters", which they saw as radiating out from Cuzco. Cuzco was both a grand, ceremonial centre and the seat of government. The emperor resided in the royal palace, while most of the common people lived outside the city on farms. Soldiers, administrators, engineers, and priests travelled to Cuzco from all over the empire to receive instructions.

❺ CIVIL WAR

In 1525, the Inca empire was engulfed in a civil war between rivals for the imperial throne. The war had inadvertently been started by Spanish invaders. They had accidentally introduced smallpox to the region. This disease killed the emperor and prompted the feud between his successors. The war was won by Atahualpa in 1532, but he didn't have long to enjoy his triumph, as Spanish invaders appeared soon after.

❻ INCA DECLINE

When the Incas and the Spanish finally met in battle in 1532, the Incas had the greater numbers. But the superior steel weapons and armour of the Spanish proved decisive, and they took the Inca emperor captive. Atahualpa tried to secure his release by offering a vast ransom of 24 tonnes of gold and silver. The Spanish gratefully accepted, before executing the emperor anyway. The empire was now effectively in Spanish hands.

❼ OWN WORST ENEMY

Logically, the Incas should have defeated the Spanish fairly easily. Despite the Spaniards' superior weaponry, the Incas vastly outnumbered the invaders. When Pizarro attacked Atahualpa, the Incas had more than 30,000 soldiers (shown here) stationed nearby. However, the rigid nature of Inca society meant that when the Spanish captured the emperor, they effectively captured the empire, because nobody else had the authority to lead.

Eighteenth-century portrait of Atahualpa, the last Inca emperor

The Spanish conquistador ("conqueror") Francisco Pizarro, who defeated the mighty Inca empire with a force of just 180 men

▶ THE SAPA INCA

Reigning at the top of Inca society was the emperor, known as the Sapa Inca. The all-powerful Sapa Inca lived a privileged life, carried everywhere by servants, eating from gold plates, and wearing the finest clothes, which would be thrown away after having been worn just once. The position of Sapa Inca was hereditary and passed on to the son.

The Sapa Inca wore headdresses of gold and feathers and was believed to be descended from the Sun god, Inti

▼ MACHU PICCHU

High in the Andes, Machu Picchu was one of the few major Inca sites to escape destruction by the Spanish in the 16th century. Built around 1450, it was abandoned shortly after the Europeans invaded. However, it was not discovered by the Spanish or the wider world until the 20th century. Explorers found the ruins of temples, palaces, homes, and terrace gardens.

▲ MASTER BUILDERS

The Incas were master builders, rapidly creating large cities as they expanded their empire. These cities were mainly used for government business. Each had a palace for the Sapa Inca. The Incas also used their building skills to increase the amount of land available for farming by creating stone-faced terraces – flat levels cut into the sides of hills.

Machu Picchu contains the only *Intihuatana* – a sacred stone dedicated to the Sun god – not to have been destroyed by the Spanish

THE INCA WORLD

The speed and ease with which the Incas built up their great empire was largely due to their supreme organizational skills. The Inca government was extremely efficient. As soon as a new territory was conquered for the empire, officials were sent out to make records of its wealth, engineers were set to work building roads to connect it, and governors were appointed to run it. The Incas were also very good farmers. This allowed them to exploit a range of different environments from the coastal lowlands to the mountain slopes of the Andes.

◀ INCA SOCIETY

Just below the Sapa Inca were the nobles, who also lived comfortable lives and were given the most important jobs in government. The lives of normal people were much harder. They had to farm the land and pay a labour tax to the state, helping to maintain the roads and build bridges. The main crops were quinoa, maize, and potatoes. They also kept llamas for wool, food, and transportation.

▲ INCA RELIGION

The Incas worshipped many different gods, which they associated with natural forces. Their main deity, however, was the Sun god, Inti. The Incas believed these gods had to be kept happy through worship. They held many religious festivals throughout the year, and these involved music, dancing, food, and sometimes human sacrifices. The Incas also mummified their dead as they believed their ancestors could contact the living through dreams, omens, and signs.

Quipus were read and interpreted by special officials called *Quipucamayocs*

▲ ROADS

The Incas built some 40,000 km (25,000 miles) of roads to link up their vast empire. The roads were not there to let the population move about but to control the empire. Their use was restricted to government officials, the army, and messengers. The Incas did not discover the wheel, so all journeys were made on foot. Roadrunners called *chasqui* carried official messages across the empire, and these were usually passed on orally from one runner to the next.

◀ ORGANIZATION

The Inca empire was a very organized place, overseen by thousands of government officials who formed part of a strict hierarchy. Decisions and laws were made by the emperor and then passed down the chain of command. These feats of organization seem particularly remarkable as the Incas had no written language. Instead, they kept records using knotted cords of llama hair known as *quipus*.

THE PUEBLO PEOPLE

The first civilization in what is now the United States developed on the Colorado Plateau in the first millennium CE. Here, people grew maize, wove baskets, and created large cliff-side settlements, known today as *pueblos*, from the Spanish for "town". The culture reached is peak in the 12th and 13th centuries, when it was probably in contact with the cultures of Mesoamerica. However, in the 14th and 15th centuries, the pueblos were abandoned, probably because of local climate change.

▼ ANCESTRAL PUEBLOANS

Nomadic hunter-gatherers settled down to farming in the southwestern United States in the eighth century CE, growing pumpkins and maize, and raising turkeys. Out of these early communities emerged the Ancestral Puebloan civilization. They lived in large, multi-roomed complexes that were built under the overhanging walls of the region's canyons and mesas (flat-topped mountains).

▼ PUEBLO BONITO

One of the largest examples of Ancestral Puebloan architecture is the Pueblo Bonito complex in New Mexico. It is made up of 650 rooms and 32 circular ceremonial centres, known as *kivas*. In places, it is up to five storeys high, and it may have been home to thousands of people. It was occupied from roughly the mid-ninth century to the mid-12th century.

▼ HOHOKAM

South of the Ancestral Puebloans, there was a similar culture, the Hohokam. They started out as hunter-gatherers, but gradually grew in sophistication. They built permanent communities, created trade routes, and developed a complex irrigation system, digging hundreds of kilometres of canals. They also made elaborate pieces of art out of shells brought from the coast.

▲ MOGOLLON

The other great prehistoric people of this region were the Mogollon. They are believed to have had close links with the peoples of Mesoamerica. Their settlement of Casa Grande (shown here) had a Mesoamerican-style ball court. The Mogollon people also made copper axes, using techniques that were probably learnt from their southern neighbours.

◀ MIMBRES

The Mogollon people living in the Mimbres Valley in New Mexico developed their own distinct culture from around 1000 CE onwards. They are particularly well known for their black and white pottery, which usually featured geometrical designs or images of people or animals, such as this bat. This pottery may have had a religious significance to the Mimbres, who often buried their dead with pots on their heads.

Ancestral Puebloan

Hohokam

Casa Grande •

Mogollon

▶ PUEBLO DECLINE

This map shows the territories of the main Pueblo people. All three cultures had declined by the time the first European settlers arrived in the 16th century. It is believed that when Pueblo building began, the climate was slightly wetter and more suitable for farming than it is now. Conditions became increasingly drier from the 14th century onwards, leading to widespread droughts and the abandonment of the area.

MOUND BUILDERS

In the first millennium BCE, the people living in the southeastern part of North America were hunter-gatherers. Although they did not farm the land or create towns, they did build large earth mounds, beneath which they buried their dead. Over the next 2,000 years these mound builders gradually grew in sophistication, creating ever larger earth structures, developing agriculture and trading networks, and eventually founding large towns.

► HOPEWELL CULTURE

By around 100 BCE, the Adena Culture had been replaced by the Hopewell Culture. The Hopewell were a more advanced people, using mounds both to bury their dead and for ceremonial purposes. They established a wide-ranging trade network and cultivated maize. But they remained hunter-gatherers, never settling down to farming or establishing true towns.

▼ ADENA CULTURE

The practice of mound-building was started in around 500 BCE by the people of the Adena Culture in the Ohio River Valley. To begin with, they laid their dead to rest beneath small, conical mounds. Over time these mounds became larger and more elaborate. The Adena were primarily hunter-gatherers, although they did cultivate some plants, including sunflowers, and created pottery.

Burial mound made by the Adena people in Miamisburg, Ohio

This snake-shaped mound was created by the Hopewell people

▼ THE EXCHANGE SYSTEM

The Hopewell people operated a network of trade routes known as the Hopewell Exchange System. At its peak, this reached from southeastern North America all the way north to what is now Canada. Most of the trade was conducted along the region's waterways. The network provided the Hopewell with exotic materials to make their art.

A Hopewell carving made from mica

Hopewell carvings of a bird's claw and a bear

▼ MISSISSIPPIAN CULTURE

The transition from hunter-gathering to settled farming was made in around 800 CE by the Mississippian Culture. They emerged in the region around the point where the Ohio and Mississippi rivers meet. The Mississippian people engaged in large-scale agriculture, farming maize extensively, and lived in settled communities and towns. They also built mounds topped by wooden temples where religious rites were performed.

▶ SOUTHERN CULT

The people of the Mississippian Culture believed the Universe was split into three levels: the Above World of the Sun, the Moon, and the gods; the Middle World where people lived; and the chaotic Underworld. These levels were linked by a giant cedar tree. This belief system was known as the Southern Cult.

This embossed copper face has facial decorations associated with the Southern Cult

▶ CAHOKIA

The largest of the Mississippian people's settlements was the city of Cahokia. Home to some 30,000 inhabitants, it contained no fewer than 120 mounds. At the centre of the city was the largest mound of all, Monk's Mound, upon which sat the great wooden palace of the city's ruler.

Wooden stairs lead up to the top of Monk's Mound

▶ DECLINE

The Mississippian Culture went into decline and Cahokia was abandoned in the 15th century for reasons that are still unknown. Over-hunting, deforestation, soil erosion, and conquest by rival peoples have all been put forward as possible explanations. Although most of the Mississippian settlements disappeared, mound-building continued in a few places, such as Natchez (shown here), until the 17th century when the first European settlers arrived.

The Emerald Mound was the main ceremonial centre of the Natchez people

NATIVE CULTURES OF NORTH AMERICA

When the first settlers from Europe arrived in North America in the 16th century, they found a continent already home to more than a million people. These were split into more than 300 tribes, speaking more than 200 languages. They had found ways to exploit the continent's natural resources all the way from the frozen north to the arid south, and had developed a rich variety of lifestyles, artistic traditions, and religious beliefs. However, contact with the Europeans, and particularly their diseases, would greatly reduce both their territory and numbers.

▶ ORIGINS

Experts believe that North America's first settlers arrived from Asia at least 12,000 years ago, during the last ice age. They may have come by boat or walked across a land bridge caused by sea levels dropping to levels much lower than they are now. These inhabitants hunted large prey, such as mammoth, and this may have contributed to these creatures becoming extinct.

▲ SHAMANS

Many Native American tribes believed the natural world was controlled by invisible forces living in the Spirit World. Special individuals, known as shamans, could channel these forces to heal the sick. Shamans also used medicinal herbs and performed healing ceremonies. Unfortunately, their skills proved largely useless against European diseases, such as smallpox.

▲ THE GRASSY PLAINS

On the great grass plains in the centre of North America, the tribes hunted buffalo. The animals provided them with food, clothes, and skins with which they made their tents, known as teepees. Prior to the arrival of Europeans with horses, the tribes followed the herds on foot, often driving the animals off the top of cliffs.

▼ CLOVIS CULTURE

The first peoples in North America hunted using spears with sharp, stone tips. Some of the earliest inhabitants have been named the Clovis people, after Clovis in New Mexico. This is the site of numerous archaeological finds, such as fluted spear points. The disappearance of the Clovis Culture may have been caused by the extinction of the large prey that they hunted.

110

Inuit weapons included harpoons, such as this one. They were made from the tusks and skins of the animals they hunted.

▲ THE FROZEN NORTH

Some tribes developed ways to live on the frozen shores of the Arctic Ocean. In around 1000 CE, the Thule Inuit, a people from Alaska, arrived in the region, and spread right along the north coast of Canada and across to Greenland. They survived by hunting large marine mammals, such as seals, walruses, and whales, and built temporary shelters, known as *aputiaks*, from blocks of snow.

▲ LONG HOUSES

Iroquois villages were filled with long, single-room buildings known as long houses. Each long house was made of bendable wooden poles and pieces of bark, and could be up to 45 m (150 ft) long. A dozen or so families might live together in a house, sharing a central fire. The Iroquois's main crops were maize, beans, and squash, which they called "The Three Sisters".

▼ FERTILE NORTHEAST

In the east and northeast, people hunted game and fished the lakes and rivers using canoes made from pieces of tree bark, sewed together with roots. In the 15th century, five rival tribes joined together to form a powerful organization, the Iroquois League. This became a dangerous opponent for the European invaders in later centuries.

ROCK ART
These Aboriginal rock paintings from the Kimberley region of Australia are thought to be 8,000 years old. They show the "Great Fish Chase" with images of various fish being hunted by indigenous Australians.

112

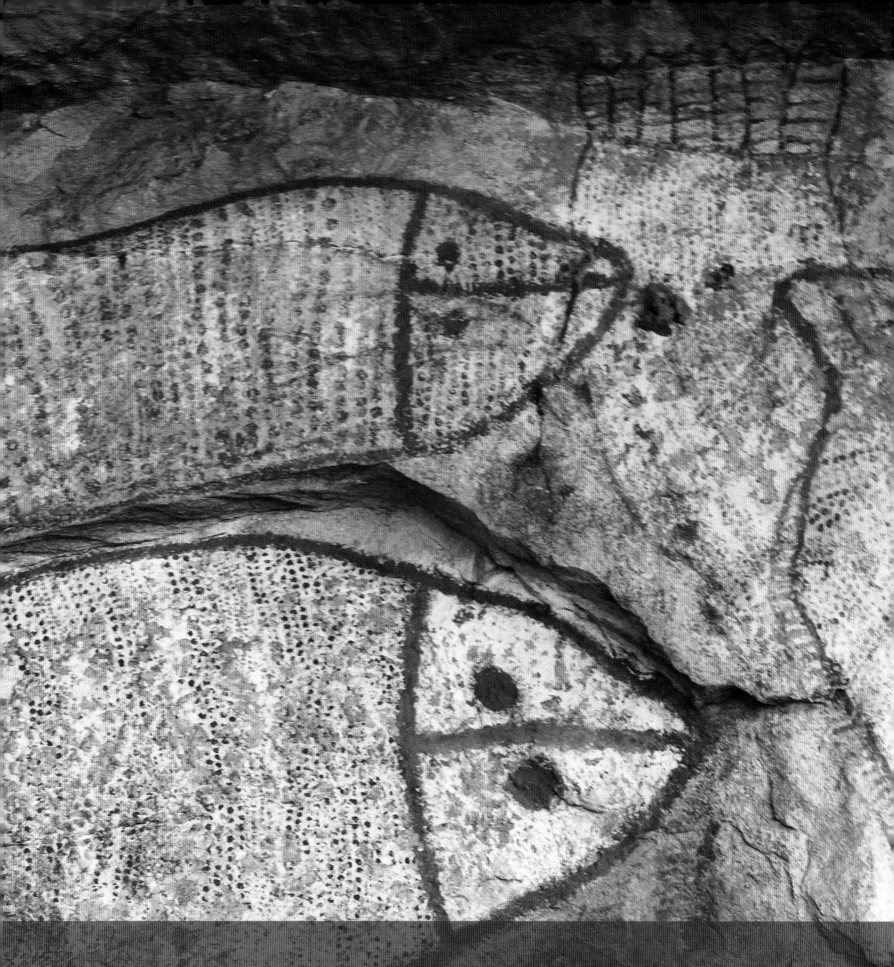

The Pacific

AUSTRALIA

Once joined to the super-continent Gondwanaland, Australia broke away around 45 million years ago and subsequently developed a unique collection of animals and plants. The history of its first peoples followed a similar pattern. For more than 40,000 years, the indigenous Australians enjoyed a largely isolated existence, free from outside influences. When the first European settlers arrived in the 18th century, there were roughly 500,000 indigenous Australians living on the continent who spoke around 300 different languages.

Coastline during the last ice age

Southeast Asia

Modern coastline

Australia

ORIGINS ▶

The first people to reach the continent came from the islands of Southeast Asia to the northwest, at least 40,000 years ago, and presumably travelled by boat. This took place during the last ice age, when sea levels were lower than they are now, which would have made the journey slightly shorter.

The largest marsupial that ever lived, the diprotodon, died out soon after humans arrived

▲ GIANT MARSUPIALS

The new arrivals in Australia were hunter-gatherers. They adapted quickly to the different environments of the vast continent, including rainforests and deserts. During the last ice age, the people shared the land with a range of large animals, including 3 m (10 ft) tall kangaroos and giant flesh-eating marsupials. It's believed that the indigenous Australians may have driven these creatures to extinction through over-hunting.

▼ SOCIAL RELATIONS

Indigenous Australians lived in family groups, which formed part of larger tribes. Tribal laws were passed down orally, as the peopled did not develop a form of writing. Aboriginal society was governed by strong ties of kinship and people were encouraged to marry outside their own family group.

Boys dancing at a festival for indigenous Australians

▼ HUNTING AND FORAGING

The people spent much of their time hunting and foraging. Women used digging sticks to uncover yams and edible roots, and collected berries and seeds, while the men hunted. They became excellent trackers, often using camouflage and mimicry to get close to their prey, which they killed with a spear or a type of curved throwing stick known as a boomerang.

▲ FIRESTICK FARMING

Although the indigenous Australians didn't develop agriculture, they did influence their environment through firestick farming. This involved burning an area of vegetation in order to create new habitats. For instance, burning scrub turned the area into grassland and encouraged the numbers of grass-eating animals, which the people then hunted.

◀ ART AND THE DREAMING

The people of the Kakadu area of northwest Australia developed a unique style known as X-Ray art, in which animals were depicted as if they were see-through. Some rock paintings may be up to 25,000 years old. The indigenous Australians also developed a religion based on another world known as "the Dreaming". They believed every person living in this world arrived from the Dreaming and returned to it when they died.

X-Ray rock painting of a fish

Rock painting of a pair of Dreaming figures

X-Ray rock painting of a turtle

▶ DINGOES

The peoples of northwest Australia formed relationships with dingoes, a type of wild dog, training them to hunt. The presence of dingoes suggests that the indigenous Australians did not remain entirely isolated from the outside world. It is believed the animals were introduced around 3500 BCE, well after the first migrations to the continent.

▼ TRIBAL AREAS

Though mainly nomadic, the indigenous Australians did settle down in semi-permanent villages in fertile areas where food was plentiful enough to allow long stays. In the dry deserts of the centre, the people moved around constantly. Even so, they maintained distinct tribal territories based on known sources of water, the most precious resource in the desert.

The water-holding frog stores fluid inside its body and can be a vital source of water in the Australian desert

THE PACIFIC ISLANDS

There are thousands of islands scattered across the enormous Pacific Ocean. The colonization of these islands, some of which are separated by thousands of kilometres of open water, was one of the great feats of human exploration. Beginning around 2000 BCE, people from Southeast Asia headed east, gradually settling island after island. By 300 BCE, three distinct groups had emerged – Melanesians, Micronesians, and Polynesians – each with their own distinct culture.

▼ NAN MADOL

The settlers of Micronesia formed themselves into tribes, led by chiefs, who became more and more powerful as time went on. In around 1200 CE, the ruling family on the Micronesian island of Pohnpei showed their authority by having a large palace, known as Nan Madol, built for themselves. It was constructed on a series of artificial offshore islands.

The palace at Nan Madol was abandoned in around 1500 when the rulers were overthrown

▶ MANA

In Pacific islander culture, *mana* was a supernatural power that dwelt in all living things, and which provided people with power and authority. The island chiefs had the most amount of mana, and they passed this on to their first-born sons. Second sons, however, received nothing. It was the desire of second sons to acquire their own mana that largely drove the colonization of new islands.

Mana could also reside in certain special artificial objects, such as this charm

Pacific Ocean

Micronesia

Melanesia

Papua New Guinea

Solomon Islands

Vanuatu

Australia

New Caledonia

The islands of Melanesia and Micronesia are spread over thousands of kilometres of the southwestern Pacific

▶ MELANESIA AND MICRONESIA

The group of islands to the north and east of Australia, now called Melanesia, were settled first in around 2000 BCE. The people here developed a form of pottery known as Lapita, which they took with them as they travelled. By studying the remains of this pottery, experts have been able to trace the migration of the culture. The islands of Micronesia, to the north of Melanesia, were the next to be settled, beginning in around 1500 BCE.

The islands of Hawaii were colonized by around 400 CE

▼ POLYNESIA

Once Melanesia and Micronesia had been colonized, the settlers headed east towards Polynesia, a remote group of more than a thousand islands spread across an enormous stretch of ocean. The discovery of Lapita pots shows that the islands of Fiji, Tonga, and Samoa were settled around 2,000 years ago. However, it would be several hundred years before the Polynesians built boats capable of travelling to the far northern and eastern islands.

Twin-hulled canoes had two equal-sized hulls held together by crossbeams

Polynesia

Hawaii

French Polynesia

Samoa

Cook Islands

Tonga

Easter Island

Fiji

New Zealand

▼ THE OUTRIGGER CANOE

The settlement of the Pacific islands was started by the invention of a special type of boat known as an outrigger canoe. The boat consisted of a main hull attached to one or more support floats. These floats made the canoe much more stable on rough water than traditional boats. It allowed the Pacific island sailors to travel farther than ever before.

▲ TWIN-HULLED CANOES

The twin-hulled canoe was the most effective long-distance sea vessel yet built. These boats were capable of travelling enormous distances, up to 4,000 km (2,500 miles) across the Pacific. A massive platform sat on top of the twin hulls carrying a colonization squad of people, food, animals, and seeds for cultivation. The canoe's invention allowed the Polynesians to reach Easter Island by about 700 CE and New Zealand some time around 1200 CE.

The outrigger is the support float that stops the canoe from capsizing in choppy weather

117

EASTER ISLAND

In 1722, a Dutch explorer became the first European to set foot on a small Pacific island thousands of kilometres from the nearest civilization. He called it Easter Island in honour of the day he arrived, although the people living there knew it as *Te Pito Te Henua*, meaning "the navel of the world". At their peak, a thriving population of thousands had practised a unique culture centred on the creation of giant stone heads. However, the island's population would be reduced to just a handful of individuals over the next few centuries.

Brazil

Bolivia

San Felix Island

San Ambrosia Island

Paraguay

Salay Gomez Island

Uruguay

Easter Island

Juan Fernandez Islands

Argentina

Chile

▶ ISOLATED ISLAND

Lying 3,510 km (2,195 miles) west of Chile and hundreds of kilometres from the nearest large island, Easter Island wasn't colonized until around the eighth century CE. According to the island's legends, the first settler was Hotu Matu'a, who arrived on a twin-hulled canoe with his wife and family.

Each head was probably moved into position on log rollers

▶ GIANT STONE HEADS

The island's society was divided into clans, led by chiefs. In around 1000 CE, a cult of ancestor worship began on the island, characterized by the carving of giant heads, known as *moai*. The clans competed to carve the biggest and most impressive moai, which they believed possessed mana (see page 116). Nearly 1,000 heads had been carved by the time the tradition came to an end.

▼ SOUTH AMERICAN CONTACT?

The presence of sweet potatoes on Easter Island has long puzzled historians. The vegetable is native to South America, many thousands of kilometres to the east, so how did it end up here? It seems likely that the Polynesians used their seafaring skills to travel to South America and back, bringing the potato with them.

▲ WRITING

The people of Easter Island developed the only indigenous form of writing in the Pacific islands. Known as *rongorongo*, it is believed to have been a religious script, written and read only by the religious elite. Just a few examples survive, carved onto wooden tablets using, according to local legend, sharks' teeth. The script is made up of picture-like symbols, including images of what appear to be birds and fish, but it has never been deciphered.

▲ DECLINE

The stone head cult came to an end in around 1500. By this time, the island's resources had begun to fail. The trees that once covered the island had all been cut down and used to transport the heads. The lack of trees led to soil erosion and agricultural collapse. Trapped on the isolated island, the people had nowhere to go and began turning on each other. The clans went to war, toppling the heads and fighting for food. From a peak of around 7,000, the population had decreased to just 2,000 by the time the first Europeans arrived.

▶ BIRDMAN OF THE YEAR

This is a carving of the *Tangata Manu*, or "birdman of the year", the central figure in a cult that arose after the fall of the statue cult. Every year, the clans would choose a candidate to swim to the nearby small island of Motu Nui to find the first egg laid by a sooty tern. Whoever won would be the "birdman" and his clan would control the island's resources for the next year.

NEW ZEALAND

The islands of New Zealand, 1,600 km (1,000 miles) from their nearest neighbours, were the last to be settled in the colonization of Polynesia. The first settlers found a forested land unlike anywhere else in Polynesia. The new inhabitants, who called themselves Maori and the island *Aotearoa*, meaning "land of the long white cloud", hunted the large birds that dominated the land.

❶ SETTLEMENT

New Zealand's first settlers arrived in around 1200 CE, making it one of the world's most recently inhabited countries. The Maori originally came from another Polynesian island, although which one is still unknown – Tahiti seems the most likely. According to Maori legends, the first settler in New Zealand was named Kupe. He arrived aboard a canoe (*waka hourua*) from his homeland of Hawaiki, having battled a giant octopus on the way.

❷ FARMING AND HUNTING

The Maori hunted and fished the islands' abundant wildlife. One of their favourite meals was a large flightless bird known as the moa, which they had driven to extinction by around 1500 CE. This also led to the demise of Haast's eagle, the largest species of eagle ever to have existed, which preyed on moas. The Maori also grew plants, such as yams, that they brought from Polynesia.

❸ WARFARE AND PA

Warfare between Maori tribes was common as chiefs tried to increase their mana, or spiritual authority. Cannibalism occasionally formed part of these conflicts, with battles sometimes ending in "feasts of the vanquished". This not only destroyed the physical bodies of the tribe's enemies, but also removed their mana. To protect themselves against attack, the tribes built fortified hilltop settlements known as *pa*. The pa was seen as the physical representation of the tribe's mana.

New Zealand is made up of two main islands, North Island and South Island

This carved figure once guarded the entrance to a pa

⑥

Pa were often protected by earthworks topped with wooden stakes

④ BODY MARKINGS

Ta Moko, the marking of the body with tattoos, was seen as an important part of Maori development, signalling the transition from childhood to adulthood. Men received tattoos on their faces, buttocks, and thighs, while women decorated their lips and chins. The tattoos were made using a chisel-like instrument, known as an *uhi*, which produced grooves in the skin.

④

⑤

⑤ TRIBES AND CHIEFS

Maori society was divided into a number of large tribes known as *iwis*. Each iwi was formed of a number of sub-tribes called *hapus*, with each lead by an *ariki*, or chief. The hapus banded together to form the iwi in times of war, but generally remained independent. Each hapu was further divided into a number of *whanaus*, or extended families. These were the basic units of Maori society.

⑥ MAORI CREATION STORY

The Maori preserved their history and myths through oral narratives. One of these stories tells how the world was created when the embrace of the Sky Father, Ranginui, with the Earth Mother, Papatuanuku, was forcefully pulled apart by their children. New Zealand itself was created when the god Maui used a jawbone to pull a mighty fish out of the sea. This fish then turned into the North Island.

TIMELINE

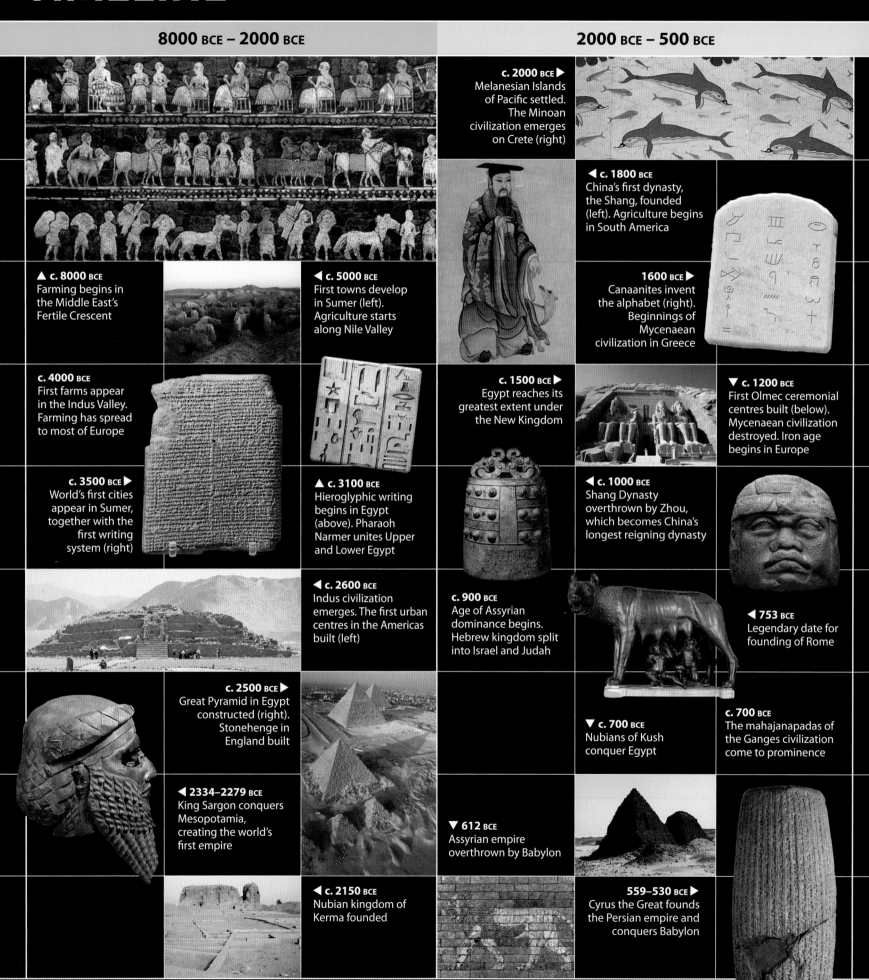

8000 BCE – 2000 BCE

▲ c. 8000 BCE
Farming begins in the Middle East's Fertile Crescent

◄ c. 5000 BCE
First towns develop in Sumer (left). Agriculture starts along Nile Valley

c. 4000 BCE
First farms appear in the Indus Valley. Farming has spread to most of Europe

c. 3500 BCE ►
World's first cities appear in Sumer, together with the first writing system (right)

▲ c. 3100 BCE
Hieroglyphic writing begins in Egypt (above). Pharaoh Narmer unites Upper and Lower Egypt

◄ c. 2600 BCE
Indus civilization emerges. The first urban centres in the Americas built (left)

c. 2500 BCE ►
Great Pyramid in Egypt constructed (right). Stonehenge in England built

◄ 2334–2279 BCE
King Sargon conquers Mesopotamia, creating the world's first empire

◄ c. 2150 BCE
Nubian kingdom of Kerma founded

2000 BCE – 500 BCE

c. 2000 BCE ►
Melanesian Islands of Pacific settled. The Minoan civilization emerges on Crete (right)

◄ c. 1800 BCE
China's first dynasty, the Shang, founded (left). Agriculture begins in South America

1600 BCE ►
Canaanites invent the alphabet (right). Beginnings of Mycenaean civilization in Greece

c. 1500 BCE ►
Egypt reaches its greatest extent under the New Kingdom

▼ c. 1200 BCE
First Olmec ceremonial centres built (below). Mycenaean civilization destroyed. Iron age begins in Europe

◄ c. 1000 BCE
Shang Dynasty overthrown by Zhou, which becomes China's longest reigning dynasty

c. 900 BCE
Age of Assyrian dominance begins. Hebrew kingdom split into Israel and Judah

◄ 753 BCE
Legendary date for founding of Rome

▼ c. 700 BCE
Nubians of Kush conquer Egypt

c. 700 BCE
The mahajanapadas of the Ganges civilization come to prominence

▼ 612 BCE
Assyrian empire overthrown by Babylon

559–530 BCE ►
Cyrus the Great founds the Persian empire and conquers Babylon

◀ **c. 500 BCE**
Celtic La Tène culture begins to dominate Europe

◀ **334–323 BCE**
Alexander the Great conquers the Persian empire

▲ **c. 700 CE**
Ancestral Puebloan farming culture thrives in North America

◀ **c. 800 CE**
Mississippian mound building culture expands in North America's eastern woodlands

321 BCE ▶
Mauryan empire founded

▼ **c. 450 BCE**
First burial mounds built by Adena people of eastern North America

c. 850–900 CE ▶
Chimú empire founded in South America. Toltec state founded at Tula. Many Maya sites decline (right)

▼ **221 BCE**
End of Warring States Period sees China unified under Qin Shi Huangdi

◀ **1000 CE**
People of Easter Island carve giant stone heads (left). Tiwanaku and Wari empires collapse

◀ **c. 200 BCE**
In South America, the first Nazca lines are mapped out (left), and Moche Culture develops

▶ **1168 CE**
Tula in Mexico is destroyed and Toltec state collapses

◀ **27 BCE**
Roman empire founded under Augustus

100 CE ▼
Tiwanaku state emerges on South America's Andean coast

◀ **c. 1300 CE**
Drought causes decline of Pueblo culture and abandonment of urban centres

▼ **c. 120 CE**
Hadrian's Wall built (below). Roman empire at greatest extent

◀ **1200 CE**
Inca state founded and goes on to take over much of the Andes

1200 CE
New Zealand settled for first time

▼ **c. 300 CE**
The Maya civilization enters its peak period

◀ **1325 CE**
Aztec empire emerges following the founding of Tenochititlán

▼ **320 CE**
Gupta empire founded (below). Classical age of India begins

350 CE
Nubian kingdom of Meroe collapses, following an attack by Axum

▲ **1450 CE**
Great Zimbabwe is abandoned (above). Mississippian mound building culture declines

▶ **476 CE**
Western Roman empire collapses

1519–1536 CE ▶
Spanish invaders conquer the Aztec empire (right) and then the Inca empire

Glossary

260-DAY CALENDAR
A calendar based on a 260-day year that was used by several Mesoamerican civilizations, including the Olmecs and the Maya.

AGRICULTURE
Farming – the process of growing crops and rearing livestock.

ARCHAEOLOGY
The study of past cultures and civilizations through the recovery and examination of buildings, artefacts, and objects that people have left behind.

BCE
"Before Common Era", used to describe the years before 1 CE.

BLOOD LETTING
Cutting or pricking oneself, or someone else, to produce blood. The blood is then given as an offering or sacrifice to a god or gods. Blood letting was widespread in the ancient civilizations of Mesoamerica and South America.

BRONZE AGE
A period in the development of civilizations characterized by the production and use of weapons and tools made from bronze. This took place at different times around the world, usually after a stone age and before an iron age.

CARAVAN
A group of vehicles or animals travelling in single file, often linked together. Camel caravans were used in ancient times to transport goods across the deserts of North Africa and the Middle East.

CAVALRY
Soldiers that fight mainly on horseback.

CE
"Common Era", used to describe the years from 1 CE to today.

CENTRALIZED
Controlled by a single authority.

CIRCUS
A circular venue surrounded by spectator seats where sporting events, such as chariot races, took place in ancient Rome.

CITIZEN
In ancient times, a citizen was a member of a particular city. Later, it meant a member of a larger state, country, or empire.

CITY-STATE
A region controlled by a city.

CIVIL SERVANTS
A group of people who work for the government.

CIVIL WAR
A conflict between different groups within the same state or region who had previously been united.

CIVILIZATION
A complex society that lives in a city, gets its food through farming, has a social hierarchy, and is ruled by a government.

CLIMATE CHANGE
Long-term variations in a region's climate. These can have profound effects on the environment and humans' ability to live there.

CODEX
A type of book made of individual sheets of material, such as bark, which are tied or bound together.

COLONY
A settlement founded by people from a particular state in another area or country. Usually, the new settlement remains loyal to, or is directly ruled by, that state.

CULTIVATION
Growing plants for food.

CULTURE
A distinct society that shares the same customs, language, and belief systems. Culture can also describe the customs themselves.

CUNEIFORM
One of the first writing systems, which was made up of symbols created by making impressions in wet clay with a reed.

DEMOCRACY
A system of government adopted in ancient Athens in which every freeborn man older than 20 years could vote on decisions.

DEMOTIC
A simplified version of the Egyptian hieroglyphic writing system.

DOMESTICATION
The taming of animals through selective breeding.

DYNASTY
A succession of rulers from the same family that maintains power for several generations.

EMPEROR
The ruler of an empire, usually a member of a hereditary dynasty.

EMPIRE
A group of states or peoples ruled by a single leader, known as the emperor or empress. Empires are usually built up through conquest.

ENLIGHTENMENT
A state of bliss, free from suffering, pain, or worry. Achieving enlightenment is the ultimate goal of followers of the Buddhist religion.

FERTILE CRESCENT
An area of land in the ancient Middle East where farming is believed to have started around 10,000 years ago.

FIEFDOM
An area controlled by a member of a royal family.

FLOOD PLAINS
The low areas either side of a river where regular flooding takes place. Many ancient civilizations, including those in Egypt, the Indus Valley, and China, emerged on flood plains.

FRESCO
A type of wall painting popular in ancient Greece and Rome, in which paint is applied directly to wet plaster and then dried.

GLYPHS
Symbols used in a writing system.

GOLIATH
A giant warrior of the Middle Eastern Philistine people. According to the Bible, Goliath was slain by the young boy David, using just a sling shot and stone.

HELLENISTIC
Something that was part of, or was influenced by, the Greek civilization that flourished around the Mediterranean, North Africa, and the Middle East between the death of Alexander the Great in 323 BCE and the emergence of the Roman empire in 27 BCE.

HEREDITARY
Something that is passed between members of the same family from one generation to the next.

HIERARCHY
The division of a people or society into groups, or classes, according to their power. For example, in ancient societies, the king would often be at the top of the hierarchy, while slaves would be at the bottom.

HIEROGLYPHICS
An Egyptian form of writing, which emerged around 3000 BCE and used pictures to represent objects, actions, and thoughts.

ICE AGE
A period when global temperatures were much lower than they are today, and icy glaciers covered much of the Earth's surface. The most recent ice age ended around 12,000 years ago.

INDIGENOUS
Original or first – the indigenous people are the first to have lived in a particular area.

INFANTRY
Soldiers that fight mainly on foot.

IRON AGE
A period in the development of civilizations characterized by the production and use of weapons and tools made from iron. This took place at different times around the world, usually after a bronze age.

IRRIGATION
To dig channels along which water can flow from a river (or other body of water) to an area of dry land.

KILN
An oven or furnace for drying and hardening clay and bricks.

MANA
A spiritual force that, according to the Pacific islanders, dwelt in all living things. It provided the chiefs with power and authority.

MESOAMERICA
An ancient region made up of Mexico and the countries of Central America where numerous civilizations developed. These included the Olmecs, the Maya, and the Aztecs.

MONARCHY
A form of government where the state is led by a monarch (the king or queen), who is usually part of a hereditary dynasty.

MONOTHEISM
Belief in a single god. Judaism, Christianity, and Zoroastrianism are all monotheistic religions.

MOSAIC
Floor decorations made using tiny pieces of glass and stone that are gradually built up to form a picture.

MUMMIFICATION
The process of preserving a dead body.

MUMMY
A preserved, dead body.

NEOLITHIC
The "New Stone Age"– the period that began with the start of farming and ended with the adoption of bronze tools and implements.

NOMADS
People who have no fixed home, but constantly travel from place to place.

PHARAOH
The supreme hereditary ruler of ancient Egypt. He or she was the equivalent of a king or emperor.

PHILOSOPHERS
People who try to work out how the world works and how people should behave. The ancient Greeks came up with the term "philosophy", which means "love of wisdom".

PILGRIMAGE
A journey to a sacred place.

PLATEAU
An area of flat land that rises up above the surrounding landscape.

POLYTHEISM
The worship of many gods. The religions of the ancient Romans, Greeks, Egyptians, Chinese, Maya, and Aztecs were all polytheistic.

POTTER'S WHEEL
A rotating disk on which clay is shaped to form pottery.

PRIEST/PRIESTESS
A person who has the authority to perform a religious ceremony and to communicate with the god (or gods) on behalf of worshippers.

PROFESSIONALS
People who are paid to do a job.

PROPAGANDA
Selectively chosen information that is used to persuade people to believe something, such as in the greatness of a particular leader or nation.

PUNIC WARS
Three wars fought between Rome and Carthage, which ended with the destruction of Carthage.

PYRAMID
A large monument with four sides, a wide base, and a narrow top. Pyramids are characteristic of the civilizations of ancient Egypt and Mesoamerica.

REPUBLIC
A type of government practised by the Roman state from 509 BCE to 27 BCE. During this period, the state was ruled by two elected leaders, known as consuls, who served for just one year. They could not stand for consecutive terms of office.

RITUAL
A ceremony (or ceremonies) that forms part of an act of worship.

SACRIFICE
To give something to the gods in return for their favour. A sacrifice could be food, precious objects, or the lives of animals and even humans. Several of the civilizations of Mesoamerica practised human sacrifice.

SEMITIC
A group of languages from the ancient Middle East and North Africa. This includes a number of related tongues, including Akkadian, Phoenician, Hebrew, Aramaic, and Arabic.

SEVEN WONDERS OF THE ANCIENT WORLD
A list compiled by Greek writers in the second century BCE of the most impressive structures and monuments known to them. The wonders were: Hanging Gardens of Babylon, Lighthouse of Alexandria, Colossus of Rhodes, Temple of Artemis at Ephesus, Mausoleum of Halicarnassus, Statue of Zeus at Olympia, and Great Pyramid of Giza – the only wonder still standing today.

SILK ROAD
Overland trade route between China, India, Central Asia, the Middle East, and Europe. It was named after the precious material, silk, which for many years was made only by the Chinese and was traded with other civilizations.

SLAVE
Someone who is owned by another person or group, and made to work for them.

SOCIETY
A group of people with a shared culture, interests, government institutions, and economic organization.

STATE
A group of people ruled by a single government. The term "state" can also be used to refer to the government.

STELE
A stone slab or column that usually bears inscriptions and is erected to commemorate a particular event.

STYLUS
A tool used for writing by making impressions on tablets. The Mesopotamians used blunt, wedge-shaped styluses to write cuneiform on clay tablets. The ancient Romans used pointed styluses to write on wax tablets.

TEMPLE
A building or place where religious ceremonies and worship take place.

TEN COMMANDMENTS
A list of ten laws that, according to the Bible, were inscribed on two stone tablets and given to the Hebrew leader, Moses, by God.

TOMB
A chamber or monument where a dead person is buried.

TRIBE
A group of people that are usually bound together by family ties or a shared culture. Tribes are typically less sophisticated than societies, with simpler forms of government and social organization. Often, tribes are nomadic or semi-nomadic.

TRIBUTE
A type of payment demanded by rulers of their subjects.

VISHNU
One of the most important gods in Hinduism. According to Hindu teachings, Vishnu is both the creator and the destroyer of the world.

ZIGGURAT
Step pyramid built from mud-bricks by several of the civilizations of the ancient Middle East, including Sumer and Babylon. On top of each pyramid was a temple.

Index

Acknowledgements

DK would like to thank:
Chris Bernstein for preparing the index.

The publisher would like to thank the following for their kind permission to reproduce their photographs:

Key:
a–above; b–below/bottom; c–centre; f–far; l–left; r–right; t–top

4 Corbis: (tl); Hemis/Patrick Frilet (clb); Frédéric Soltan (tr); Paul Souders (crb). **5 Corbis:** Dave G. Houser (cr). **6-7 Corbis. 8 Dorling Kindersley:** The British Museum, London (crb); Pitt Rivers Museum, University of Oxford (clb). **8-9 Getty Images:** CGIBackgrounds.com (Background). **9 akg-images:** Erich Lessing (bl). **Alamy Images:** Peter Horree (bc). **Corbis:** David Lees (ca); Gianni Dagli Orti (cra). **Dreamstime.com:** Adelie Peng (cla/Doors). **iStockphoto.com:** Michael Major (cla); Les Palenik (br). **10 Corbis:** Gianni Dagli Orti (bl). **Dorling Kindersley:** Judith Miller / Ancient Art (br). **Getty Images:** De Agostini Picture Library/M. Carrieri (tr). **10-11 iStockphoto.com:** Elena Schweitzer (Building Blocks). **11 akg-images:** Erich Lessing (tl). **Alamy Images:** The Art Archive (cra). **Dorling Kindersley:** The British Museum, London (br). **Getty Images:** De Agostini Picture Library/A. de Gregorio (cl). **12 Corbis:** Gianni Dagli Orti (tr) (c). **Getty Images:** The Bridgeman Art Library/Ashmolean Museum, University of Oxford (br). **12-13 iStockphoto.com:** Sacha Bloor (Sand); Francine Freeman (Scroll). **13 Dorling Kindersley:** The British Museum, London (tl). **Getty Images:** De Agostini Picture Library (c). **14 Alamy Images:** The Art Archive (clb). **Corbis:** The Art Archives (c). **Getty Images:** The Bridgeman Art Library (br); De Agostini Picture Library (tr). **iStockphoto.com:** Mark Wragg (bl/Hand). **14-15 iStockphoto.com:** (Background); Stephen Rees (Cards). **15 The Bridgeman Art Library:** The Stapleton Collection (tl) (tr). **Corbis:** The Gallery Collection (br); PoodlesRock (bl). **Getty Images:** Gallo Images/Danita Delimont (ca). **16 Alamy Images:** INTERFOTO (bc). **Dorling Kindersley:** The British Museum, London (c). **iStockphoto.com:** (br); Felix Alim (cl); David Bronson Glover (tl). **17 akg-images:** Rabatti - Domingie (tr/Cuneiform). **Corbis:** Gianni Dagli Orti (cla/Stele). **iStockphoto.com:** AquaColor (tr/Medal); Dan Chippendale (bc/Rosettes); Eric's Photography (cla/Trophy); Michal Rozanski (tl); Perttu Sironen (bl). **18 Corbis:** Robert Harding World Imagery/Godong (cla). **Getty Images:** The Bridgeman Art Library (bc). **iStockphoto.com:** Jill Fromer (br/Tablet); Tamer Yazici (bc/Frame). **18-19 Getty Images:** The Bridgeman Art Library (cl). **iStockphoto.com:** Claudio Arnese (Background Crates); Aleksejs Polakovs (Warehouse). **19 akg-images:** (cl). **Alamy Images:** The Art Archive (c). **Corbis:** Arte & Immagini slr (tc). **Getty Images:** The Bridgeman Art Library (br). **iStockphoto.com:** (cl/Frame); Royce DeGrie (c/Wood Background); Michal Rozanski (br/Frame); Nathan Till (bl/Crate). **20 Dorling Kindersley:** The British Museum, London (c/Map). **Getty Images:** AFP/François Guillot (clb); SSPL (crb/Ship). **iStockphoto.com:** blackred (crb/Ship); Ida Jarosova (tr); Tarek El Sombati (tl). **20-21 iStockphoto.com:** (Background). **21 Corbis:** Yves Forestier (crb); David Lees (bl); Gianni Dagli Orti (ca). **Dorling Kindersley:** The British Museum, London (tr). **Getty Images:** Iconica/Jeffrey Coolidge (b/Book). **22 Corbis:** Bettmann (cb); Charles & Josette Lenars (tr); Brian A. Vikander (cl). **Dorling Kindersley:** The British Museum, London (crb). **23 akg-images:** (c). **Alamy Images:** The Art Gallery Collection (tr). **Corbis:** (cl). **Getty Images:** OJO Collection/Tom Merton (b). **24 The Bridgeman Art Library:** University Library, Leipzig/Archives Charmet (cl). **Corbis:** Sygma/Frédéric Soltan (bc). **Getty Images:** The Image Bank/Frank Krahmer (c). **24-25 Getty Images:** Axiom Photographic Agency/Marc Jackson (b/Background); Photographer's Choice/Nash Photos (t/Background). **25 Corbis:** Sandro Vannini (cl). **Dorling Kindersley:** National Maritime Museum, London (cr). **Getty Images:** De Agostini Picture Library/G. Nimatallah (cr); Robert Harding World Imagery/Sergio Pitamitz (fcl). **26-27 Corbis:** Hemis/Patrick Frilet. **28 akg-images:** Philippe Maillard (bc). **Corbis:** Gianni Dagli Orti (c); Sandro Vannini (cla). **Dorling Kindersley:** The British Museum, London (c). **28-29 Dorling Kindersley:** The British Museum, London (Senet). **iStockphoto.com:** Shirly Friedman (Papyrus). **29 Corbis:** JAI/Jon Arnold (ca); Sandro Vannini (tc); Werner Forman (bl). **Getty Images:** AFP/Oliver Lang (cb); De Agostini Picture Library/S. Vannini (cra); Stone/Richard Passmore (cr). **30 Corbis:** Charles & Josette Lenars (br); Sandro Vannini (bc). **Dorling Kindersley:** The British Museum, London (bl). **30-31 Getty Images:** Digital Vision/Artifacts Images (c/Port Hole). **iStockphoto.com:** Selahattin Bayram (b/Shelf); David Joyner (c/View). **31 Corbis:** (br); Burstein Collection (bl); José Fuste Raga (tr). **Dorling Kindersley:** The British Museum, London (ca) (cb). **32 Corbis:** Wolfgang Kaehler (fbr); Sandro Vannini (fcr). **Dorling Kindersley:** The British Museum, London (fbl); De Agostini Picture Library/A. Dagli Orti (cr). **Getty Images:** De Agostini Picture Library/G. Dagli Orti (fcl) (bl); Glowimages (cl). **32-33 Corbis:** Gianni Dagli Orti (Screen Background). **Dreamstime.com:** (iPad). **Getty Images:** Brand X Pictures/John Block (Hands). **33 The Art Archive:** Musée du Louvre, Paris/Jacqueline Hyde (cl). **Corbis:** Bojan Brecelj (br); Christine Osborne (cr); Sandro Vannini (fcr). **Getty Images:** The Bridgeman Art Library (bl). **34 Corbis:** Robert Harding World Imagery (crb). **Dorling Kindersley:** The British Museum, London (tl). **Getty Images:** Workbook Stock/Frederic Neema (tc). **34-35 Corbis:** Robert Harding World Imagery (cb); Kazuyoshi Nomachi (tc). **35 Corbis:** Gianni Dagli Orti (cr). **Dorling Kindersley:** The British Museum, London (cl) (cb); Egyptian Museum, Cairo (crb). **Getty Images:** The Bridgeman Art Library (tr). **36 Corbis:** National Geographic Society (br). **Getty Images:** Robert Harding World Imagery/Andrew McConnell (cr). **36-37 Getty Images:** Photographer's Choice/Grant Faint (r/Stand); Photolibrary/Ariadne Van Zandbergen (l). **37 Corbis:** JAI/Nigel Pavitt (br); Gianni Dagli Orti (tr). **Getty Images:** De Agostini Picture Library (cr). **38 Corbis:** Gianni Dagli Orti (crb). **Getty Images:** Comstock Images/Thinkstock (tr/Ferris Wheel). **iStockphoto.com:** Johnny Greig (ca/Lights). **38-39 iStockphoto.com:** Jason Ganser (c). **39 Corbis:** José Fuste Raga (bl). **Dreamstime.com:** Bert Folsom (bc/Hammer). **Getty Images:** The Bridgeman Art Library (br); SuperStock (cl). **40 Corbis:** Robert Harding World Imagery (bc/Tower). **Getty Images:** Photolibrary/John Cooke (bl/Fly) (bc/Rock). **iStockphoto.com:** Nina Shannon (bl/Rock). **40-41 Corbis:** Cordaiy Photo Library Ltd/Colin Hoskins (t). **iStockphoto.com:** Bartosz Hadyniak (b/Grass). **41 Alamy Images:** Images of Africa Photobank (br/Main Enclosure). **Dorling Kindersley:** The British Museum, London (cr); Natural History Museum, London (bl). **iStockphoto.com:** Don Nichols (br/Rock). **42-43 Corbis:** Frédéric Soltan. **44 Corbis:** Ecoscene/Sally A. Morgan (br); Keren Su (c). **Dreamstime.com:** (Background) (r/Wood); Martjin Mulder (br/Metal Disc); Olivier Le Queinec (cra/Nail). **Werner Forman Archive:** Moravian Museum (cra). **45 Corbis:** The Art Archive (cb); EPA/Peter Endig (clb); Arne Hodalic (c); Pete Leonard (Background). **Dorling Kindersley:** Museum of London (crb); University Museum of Archaeology and Athropology, Cambridge (cr). **46 Getty Images:** De Agostini Picture Library (bc); Photographer's Choice/Guy Vanderelst (cl); Stone+/Tim Flach (cr). **iStockphoto.com:** OPIS (c/Torches). **46-47 iStockphoto.com:** (Background). **47 Alamy Images:** WaterFrame (clb). **Corbis:** Gian Berto Vanni (tl); Roger Wood (ca). **Getty Images:** De Agostini Picture Library (br). **iStockphoto.com:** Ali Altug Kirisoglu (bc). **48 Corbis:** National Geographic Society (c). **Dorling Kindersley:** National War Museum, Athens (cr). **Getty Images:** De Agostini Picture Library/G. Nimatallah (tc); Robert Harding World Imagery/James Green (cl). **iStockphoto.com:** Mark Wragg (c/Dish). **48-49 iStockphoto.com:** Cardoni Gianluca (Plates). **49 Corbis:** Christie's Images (cr); Hemis/Bruno Morandi (tl); North Carolina Museum of Art (fcr). **Dorling Kindersley:** The British Museum, London (crb). **50-51 Getty Images:** Manuel Cohen (Temple). **51 Corbis:** Fine Art Photographic Library (crb); The Gallery Collection (c); Vanni Archive (fcr). **Dorling Kindersley:** The British Museum, London/Nick Nicholls (bc) (br). **Getty Images:** The Bridgeman Art Library (cl); De Agostini Picture Library (cr). **52 Corbis:** Araldo de Luca (crb) (br); Jodice Mimmo (fbl). **Getty Images:** Archive Photos (cr); The Image Bank/Louis-Laurent Grandadam (bl). **52-53 Dreamstime.com:** Ailenn (Background). **53 Corbis:** Bettmann (cr); Science Faction/Louie Psihoyos (br). **Getty Images:** The Bridgeman Art Library (cl). **54 Corbis:** Bettmann (cb); Robert Harding World Imagery (br). **Hoberman Collection** (cl). **54-55 Getty Images:** Photodisc/Fototeca Storica Nazionale (c/Map). **iStockphoto.com:** David Kerkhoff (Background Leather); Bill Noll (Background Wood). **55 Getty Images:** De Agostini Picture Library (cb); John-Patrick Morarescu (cr). **iStockphoto.com:** Pixhook (br). **56 Corbis:** (bc); The Art Archive (tl). **56-57 Getty Images:** Panoramic Images (Background). **57 akg-images:** (tc). **Alamy Images:** The Art Gallery Collection (bc); INTERFOTO (cla). **Corbis:** Araldo de Luca (tr). **Getty Images:** The Bridgeman Art Library (cr). **iStockphoto.com:** Tamer Yazici (cr/Frame). **58 Corbis:** Bettmann (tc) (crb); Vittoriano Rastelli (tr). **Getty Images:** Photographer's Choice/Jochem D. Wijnands (bc). **iStockphoto.com:** (bc/Camera); Arthur Domagala (bl/Cable). **58-59 iStockphoto.com:** Pavlen (Computer). **59 Corbis:** Eye Ubiquitous/Paul Seheult (tl); Araldo de Luca (tr). **Dorling Kindersley:** Courtesy of English Heritage/Joe Cornish (ftl). **Getty Images:** The Bridgeman Art Library (ftr); The Image Bank/Ed Freeman (cb); Robert Harding World Imagery/G.R. Richardson (bc). **60 Getty Images:** Robert Harding World Imagery/C. Gascoigne (cl). **60-61 Dreamstime.com:** Nikolais (Book). **Getty Images:** De Agostini Picture Library (c/Map); Panoramic Images (Background). **iStockphoto.com:** Rudyanto Wijaya (Hands). **61 Corbis:** The Art Archive (tl); Atlantide Phototravel (bc); Araldo de Luca (cl); Roger Ressmeyer (clb). **62 Dorling Kindersley:** Courtesy of the Order of the Black Prince/Geoff Dann (br). **62-63 Corbis:** Robert Harding World Imagery/James Emmerson (Background). **63 Dorling Kindersley:** The British Museum, London/Christi Graham and Nick Nicholls (cr). **Getty Images:** The Bridgeman Art Library (cl); Fuse (fcr). **64-65 Corbis:** Eye Ubiquitous/Andy Butler (Background). **65 akg-images:** Erich Lessing (cl). **Corbis:** Robert Harding World Imagery/Last Refuge (cb); Historical Picture Archive (tr); Hoberman Collection (c/Coin); Werner Forman (bc). **Dorling Kindersley:** The British Museum, London/Alan Hills (cr/Torc). **Getty Images:** De Agostini Picture Library/E. Lessing (br); Photodisc/Don Farrall (c/Treasure Chest). **iStockphoto.com:** W.P. Chambers (tr/Canvas). **66-67 Corbis:** Paul Souders. **68 Corbis:** Diego Lezama Orezzoli (bl). **Dorling Kindersley:** Courtesy of the National Museum, New Delhi/Andy Crawford (cl). **Getty Images:** De Agostini Picture Library/G. Nimatallah (cr) (ca/Coffee Stain) (cr/Folders). **iStockphoto.com:** (ca/Folder); Diane Diederich (bl/Folders); Jenny Horne (ca/Coffee Cup). **68-69 iStockphoto.com:** Bill Noll (Desk). **69 The Art Archive:** The British Library, London (cra). **Corbis:** Historical Picture Archive (crb); Luca I. Tettoni (clb); WIN-Images (bl). **Getty Images:** Brand X Pictures/Brian Hagiwara (br); Photodisc/Ryan McVay (tc). **70 Getty Images:** Hulton Archive (tr). **70-71 Getty Images:** Photolibrary/Mike Powles (Background). **iStockphoto.com:** JVT (Pillars). **71 iStockphoto.com:** Pradeep Kumar (r). **72 Alamy Images:** Robert Harding Picture Library Ltd (tc). **Corbis:** Alison Wright (crb). **Dorling Kindersley:** The British Museum, London/J. Kershaw (c) (fbl); National Museum, New Delhi (bl). **Getty Images:** The Image Bank/Martin Child (br) (crb/Frame). **iStockphoto.com:** Tobias Helbig (tc/Frame). **72-73 iStockphoto.com:** Graham Klotz (Wall); Mario Savoia (Shelves); Jyoti Thakur (l). **73 Alamy Images:** Dinodia Images (tr). **The Bridgeman Art Library:** Giraudon (c). **74 Corbis:** (ca); Asian Art & Archaeology, Inc. (cl); Werner Forman (cb). **Getty Images:** Stockbyte (bl). **74-75 Corbis:** Reuters/Mike Segar (Auction Room). **iStockphoto.com:** (Picture Frames). **75 Corbis:** Burstein Collection (ca); Royal Ontario Museum (tc). **Getty Images:** AFP/Ben Stansall (bl) (bl/Lao Zi); The Bridgeman Art Library (cla). **iStockphoto.com:** (cl). **76 Alamy Images:** The Art Archive (cra/Qin Shi); EPA/Kay Nietfeld (c). **Corbis:** EPA/Miguel Menéndez (cl); Reuters/Daniel Munoz (r). **Getty Images:** The Bridgeman Art Library (c/Sun Tzu). **iStockphoto.com:** (c/Parchment) (cra/Parchment); Wojtek Kryczka (cl/Parchment). **76-77 Corbis:** José Fuste Raga (Background). **iStockphoto.com:** Klemens Wolf (Shelf). **77 Alamy Images:** The Art Gallery Collection (cla). **Corbis:** Reuters/Daniel Munoz (c) (r); Royal Ontario Museum (cr). **Getty Images:** Glowimages (clb). **iStockphoto.com:** (clb/Parchment); Clayton Hansen (cla/Parchment). **78 Alamy Images:** The Art Archive (tr); INTERFOTO (cla); The British Museum, London/Museum of Mankind/Geoff Brightling (cb). **Dorling Kindersley:** The British Museum, London/David Gower (clb). **iStockphoto.com:** Bezmaski (tr/Kite). **78-79 iStockphoto.com:** Loic Bernard (b). **79 The Art Archive:** Genius of China Exhibition (cb). **Dorling Kindersley:** Science Museum, London/John Lepine (clb). **Dreamstime.com:** Dropu (tl). **iStockphoto.com:** Viorika Prikhodko (clb/Kite); Kriss Russell (r/Kite). **80 The Bridgeman Art Library:** Hanyang University Museum, South Korea (tl). **Werner Forman Archive:** Central History Museum, P'Yongyang, North Korea (c). **80-81 iStockphoto.com:** Felix Möckel (Jigsaw); Bill Noll (Table). **81 Alamy Images:** David Parker (br). **Corbis:** Carmen Redondo (bl); Reuters/Korea News Service (tr). **Dorling Kindersley:** Gonju National Museum, Chungcheongnam-do, South Korea (cla). **82 Corbis:** Sakamoto Photo Research Laboratory (bl) (cb). **82-83 Getty Images:** Amana Images/Keizou Wada (Background). **83 Corbis:** Sakamoto Photo Research Laboratory (clb). **Getty Images:** Photographer's Choice/Murat Taner (cra). **84 Alamy Images:** Gezmen (crb). **Getty Images:** De Agostini Picture Library (tr); Gallo Images/Danita Delimont (clb). **84-85 Corbis:** Keren Su (Flags & Yurts). **Dreamstime.com:** Stephane Duchateau (Background). **85 Alamy Images:** North Wind Picture Archives (crb). **Corbis:** Bettmann (tr) (cb). **88 Alamy Images:** David Hilbert (cl). **Corbis:** Reuters/Daniel Aguilar (bl). **Dreamstime.com:** (tr). **iStockphoto.com:** Nuno Silva (fbl). **88-89 iStockphoto.com:** Nicholas Belton (Blueprints); Vladimir (Background). **89 Corbis:** Danny Lehman (cra); Gianni Dagli Orti (crb); Werner Forman (clb). **Getty Images:** De Agostini Picture Library/Chomon-Perino (cla). **iStockphoto.com:** (tl/Paint Sample); Adem Demir (tl/Compass) (bl); Zoran Kolundzija (bc); Vasko Miokovic (tc). **90 Corbis:** Yann Arthus-Bertrand (clb); Charles & Josette Lenars (br). **Getty Images:** De Agostini Picture Library (ca). **iStockphoto.com:** Scott Hailstone (l). **90-91 Getty Images:** Stone/Paul Souders (t/Jungle Background). **iStockphoto.com:** (Stone Blocks); Enviromantic (Vines); Oleg Karpov (ca/Moss). **91 Corbis:** EPA/Francisco Martin (cb). **Dorling Kindersley:** Courtesy of the Royal Museum of Scotland, Edinburgh/Andy Crawford (ca). **Getty Images:** De Agostini Picture Library (tl); Panoramic Images (b). **92 Corbis:** EPA/Jorge Gonzalez (bl); Visions of America/Joseph Sohm (br). **92-93 Getty Images:** The Image Bank/Macduff Everton (Background). **93 Alamy Images:** Peter Horree (bc). **Corbis:** José Fuste Raga (clb); Hans Georg Roth (bl). **Getty Images:** Glow Images (ca). **94 Corbis:** Gianni Dagli Orti (c) (bc). **Getty Images:** De Agostini Picture Library (tr). **94-95 Getty Images:** The Image Bank/Jason Hawkes (Algae). **iStockphoto.com:** (Wood); Selahattin Bayram (Water); Robert Bremec (c); Mat Ferhat (Soil); Darren Wise (Mat Texture). **95 Corbis:** Bettmann (bl). **Getty Images:** Roger Viollet Collection (cb). **96 The Art Archive:** The Bodleian Library, University of Oxford (cl). **Corbis:** Bettmann (cra); Gianni Dagli Orti (bc). **96-97 Getty Images:** Martin Ruegner (bl/Cactus). **97 Corbis:** National Geographic Society (clb); Werner Forman (cr) (bc). **Getty Images:** The Bridgeman Art Library (cla); De Agostini Picture Library/G. Dagli Orti (tc). **iStockphoto.com:** Duncan Purvey (c/Cactus). **98 Corbis:** Ric Ergenbright (crb); Reuters/Mariana Bazo (cra). **Getty Images:** De Agostini Picture Library/G. Dagli Orti (c). **99 Corbis:** Bowers Museum of Cultural Art (ca). **Getty Images:** AFP/Claudio Santana (bc); De Agostini Picture Library/G. Dagli Orti (cr). **100 Corbis:** Bettmann (cr); Kevin Schafer (c). **Getty Images:** Photographer's Choice/Peter Dazeley (l/Potter). **100-101 Getty Images:** Taxi/Andreas Kuehn (Pots). **101 Corbis:** Francis G. Mayer (bc); Gianni Dagli Orti (cl); Keren Su (tc). **Getty Images:** The Bridgeman Art Library (cl); Photographer's Choice/Tom Till (tr). **102 Corbis:** Dave G. Houser (cb); Daniel Lainé (crb). **Getty Images:** Glowimages (br/Llama); Photodisc/Karl Weatherly (cl/Llama); Workbook Stock/DreamPictures (c/Llama). **102-103 Getty Images:** Gallo Images/Travel Ink (Blankets); Robert Harding World Imagery/Richard Maschmeyer (cb); Workbook Stock/DreamPictures (Background). **103 Corbis:** Brooklyn Museum (clb). **Getty Images:** De Agostini Picture Library/G. Dagli Orti (crb); Hulton Archive (cb). **104 Getty Images:** Glowimages (cl); The Image Bank/Tim Graham (c); Stockbyte (tc). **104-105 Getty Images:** Digital Vision/Michael Freeman (Background). **105 Corbis:** Gianni Dagli Orti (bc). **Getty Images:** AFP/Michael Latz (cra); Fotosearch (tc). **106 Corbis:** Tom Bean (bl); Richard A. Cooke (cl) (br). **106-107 Dreamstime.com:** (Background Stamps). **iStockphoto.com:** Matt Knannlein (Franking Marks); David Mingay (Stamp Template); Maria Toutoudaki (Album). **107 Corbis:** Arcaid/Natalie Tepper (cra); Richard A. Cooke (tl); Tetra Images (crb/Tweezers). **Getty Images:** Michael Hitoshi (b/Magnifying Glass). **iStockphoto.com:** (b/Postcard). **108 The Art Archive:** NGS Image Collection/W. Langdon Kihn (bl). **Corbis:** Richard A. Cooke (cla) (bc) (clb) (cr); Nativestock Pictures/Marilyn Angel Wynn (tc). **108-109 iStockphoto.com:** (Holes) (Concrete); Bill Noll (Grass); Linda Steward (Golf Flags). **109 Corbis:** Richard A. Cooke (cl); JAI/Walter Bibikow (crb); Werner Forman (tr). **Getty Images:** Image Source (bl/Balls); Photodisc/Philip Nealey (b). **iStockphoto.com:** Holly Kuchera (br/Stand). **110 Corbis:** Warren Morgan (br); PoodlesRock (cra). **Getty Images:** The Bridgeman Art Library (cl); MPI (cb). **110-111 iStockphoto.com:** (Tacks); Bill Noll (c/Paper); Mark Wragg (Noticeboard). **111 Corbis:** (tr) (br). **Dorling Kindersley:** Courtesy of the Town Docks Museum, Hull/Frank Greenaway (t). **Getty Images:** Nativestock/Marilyn Angel Wynn (cr). **iStockphoto.com:** Stephen Mulcahey (tl/Label). **112-113 Corbis:** Dave G. Houser. **114 Getty Images:** De Agostini Picture Library (cla). **114-115 Corbis:** Ludo Kuipers (bc). **iStockphoto.com:** (Wall). **115 Corbis:** Frank Lane Picture Agency/Chris Mattison (bc); Penny Tweedie (tl) (tc). **Getty Images:** Robert Harding World Imagery/Robert Francis (cr) (bc/Boat) (cr/Boat). **116 Corbis:** Dennis Marsico (cl/Boat); Douglas Peebles (cr). **117 Corbis:** Rob Howard (br); Dennis Marsico (cr/Boat); Anders Ryman (cl/Boat). **Getty Images:** National Geographic/Herbert Kawainui Kane (cr). **118 Getty Images:** Iconica/Buena Vista Images (clb); The Image Bank/Chris Sattlberger (bl); Photographer's Choice/Michael Dunning (br); Image Source (b/Desks). **118-119 Getty Images:** The Image Bank/Blaise Hayward (t/Blackboard). **119 Corbis:** O. Alamany & E. Vicens (tr); James L. Amos (br). **Getty Images:** Iconica/Buena Vista Images (clb); Workbook Stock/Manfred Gottschalk (cl). **120 Corbis:** George Steinmetz (br). **Getty Images:** The Bridgeman Art Library (cr); Universal Images Group/Planet Observer (bl). **120-121 Getty Images:** Time & Life Pictures/Ted Thai (c/Gateway) (r/Wooden Flap). **iStockphoto.com:** José Juan Garcia (l/Wooden Flap); Dean Turner (t/Sky). **121 Getty Images:** The Bridgeman Art Library (tl); Hulton Archive (c); Photographer's Choice/Jon Warburton Lee (c/Fence). **122 akg-images:** Rabatti - Domingie (3500 BCE) (612 BCE). **Corbis:** (753 BCE); Burstein Collection (1000 BCE); David Lees (5000 BCE); Danny Lehman (1200 BCE); Gianni Dagli Orti (2334-2279 BCE); Reuters/Mariana Bazo (2600 BCE); Sandro Vannini (3100) (559-530 BCE). **Dorling Kindersley:** The British Museum, London (8000 BCE). **Getty Images:** De Agostini Picture Library (700 BCE); Robert Harding World Imagery/Andrew McConnell (2150 BCE); Photographer's Choice/Guy Vanderelst (2000 BCE); Stone/Richard Passmore (1500 BCE); Workbook Stock/Frederic Neema (2500 BCE). **123 Alamy Images:** Images of Africa Photobank (1450 CE). **Corbis:** Arcaid/Natalie Tepper (1300 CE); Yann Arthus-Bertrand (300 CE) (1325 CE) (1519-1536 CE) (476 CE); Bettmann (27 BCE) (800 CE); Richard A. Cooke (700 CE); EPA/Miguel Menéndez (221 BCE); Hoberman Collection (334-323 BCE); Nativestock Pictures/Marilyn Angel Wynn (450 BCE); José Fuste Raga (1168 CE). **Dorling Kindersley:** The British Museum, London/J. Kershaw (320 CE); Courtesy of English Heritage/Joe Cornish (1200 CE). **Getty Images:** The Bridgeman Art Library (100 CE); Panoramic Images (850-900 CE); Photographer's Choice/Michael Dunning (1000 CE); Photographer's Choice/Tom Till (200 BCE); Stockbyte (1200 CE). **iStockphoto.com:** Pradeep Kumar (321 CE)

For further information see:
www.dkimages.com